Recent Photo of the Author

ESSENTIALS FOR FURTHER ADVANCEMENT

A FALUN GONG PRACTITIONER'S GUIDE

LI HONGZHI

FAIR WINDS
PRESS
GLOUCESTER, MASSACHUSETTES

Published in the United States of America by
Fair Winds Press
33 Commercial Street
Gloucester, Massachusetts 01930-5089

ISBN 1-931412-54-5

10 9 8 7 6 5 4 3 2 1

Cover Design: Linda Kosarin

Printed in Canada

Contents

Falun Dafa

Essentials for Further Advancement

Li Hongzhi

Lunyu[1]

The BUDDHA FA[2] is most profound; it is the most intricate and extraordinary science of all theories in the world. In order to explore this domain, people must fundamentally change their conventional human notions. Failing that, the truth of the universe will forever remain a mystery to humankind, and everyday people will forever crawl within the boundaries set by their own ignorance.

So what exactly is this BUDDHA FA, then? A religion? A philosophy? It is understood as such only by "modernized scholars of Buddhism." They merely study it on a theoretical level, regarding it as something that falls within the domain of philosophy for critical studies and so-called research. In actuality, the BUDDHA FA is not limited to the little portion in the sutras, which is only the BUDDHA FA at an elementary level. From particles and molecules to the universe, from the even smaller to the even greater, the BUDDHA FA offers insight into all mysteries, encompassing everything and

---

[1] Lunyu (loon-yew)—"An explanation using language."

[2] Fa (fah)—"Law," "Way," or "Principles."

omitting nothing. It is the nature of the universe, Zhen-Shan-Ren,[3] expressed in different ways at different levels. It is also what the Dao School calls the Dao,[4] and what the Buddha School calls the Fa.

No matter how advanced the science of today's humankind may be, it can only account for part of the universe's mysteries. Once we mention specific phenomena of the BUDDHA FA, there are people who will say: "We're now in the electronic age, and science is so advanced. Spaceships have flown to other planets, but you're still talking about these old superstitions." To be frank, no matter how advanced computers may be, they are no match for the human brain, which remains an enigma to this day. Regardless of how far spaceships may travel, they still cannot fly beyond this physical dimension in which our human race exists. What can be understood with today's human knowledge is still extremely shallow and limited—it is nowhere near a genuine understanding of the true nature of the universe. Some people do not even dare to face up to, approach, or acknowledge the facts of phenomena that objectively exist, all because these people are too conservative and are unwilling to change their conventional notions when thinking. Only the BUDDHA FA can completely unveil the mysteries of the universe, space-time, and the human body. It can truly distinguish the kind from the wicked, the good from the bad, and it can dispel all misconceptions while providing a correct understanding of things.

The guiding principles of today's human science confine its

---

[3] Zhen-Shan-Ren (juhn-shahn-ren)—Zhen means "Truth, Truthfulness"; Shan, "Compassion, Benevolence, Kindness, Goodness"; Ren, "Forbearance, Tolerance, Endurance, Self-Control."

[4] Dao (dow)—"the Way" (also spelled "Tao"); this term can also refer to one who has "attained the Dao."

development and research to this physical world, as a subject will not be studied until it is acknowledged—it follows this path. As for phenomena that are intangible and invisible, but objectively existing and reflected into our physical world as real manifestations, they are avoided and treated as inexplicable phenomena. Stubborn people have, on unsubstantiated grounds, entrenched themselves in their argument that these are just "natural" phenomena. People with ulterior motives have acted against their own consciences by labeling all these phenomena as superstitions. People with unprobing minds have shied away from these matters with the excuse that science is not sufficiently advanced to deal with them. Humankind will make a leap forward if it can take a fresh look at itself and the universe, changing its rigid mindset. The BUDDHA FA can provide people with insight into immeasurable and boundless worlds. Throughout the ages, only the BUDDHA FA has been able to completely explain human beings, the various dimensions of material existence, life, and the entire universe.

Li Hongzhi
June 2, 1992

Wealth with Virtue

The ancients said, "Money is something external to this physical body." Everyone knows it, yet everyone pursues it. A young man seeks it to satisfy his desires; a young woman wants it for glamour and luxury; an elderly person goes after it to take care of himself in his old age; a learned person desires it for his reputation; a public official fulfills his duty for it, and so on. Thus, everybody pursues it.

3

Some people even compete and fight for it; those who are aggressive take risks for it; hot-tempered people resort to violence for it; jealous people might die for it in anger. It is the duty of the ruler and officials to bring wealth to the populace, yet promotion of money-worship is the worst policy one could adopt. Wealth without virtue (*de*) will harm all sentient beings, while wealth with virtue is what all people hope for. Therefore, one cannot be affluent without promoting virtue.

Virtue is accrued from past lives. Becoming a king, an official, wealthy, or nobility all come from virtue. No virtue, no gain; the loss of virtue denotes the loss of everything. Thus, those who seek power and wealth must first accumulate virtue. By suffering hardships and doing good deeds, one can accumulate virtue among the masses. To achieve this, one must understand the principle of cause and effect. Knowing this can enable officials and the populace to exercise self-restraint, and prosperity and peace will thereby prevail under heaven.

Li Hongzhi
January 27, 1995

Broad and Profound

The Fa and principles of Falun Dafa[5] can provide guidance for anyone's cultivation practice, including for one's religious belief. This is the principle of the universe, the true Fa that has never been taught. People in the past were not allowed to know this universe's principle (the Buddha Fa). It transcends all academic theories and moral principles of human society from ancient times to this day. What was taught by religions and what people experienced in the past were only superficialities and shallow phenomena. Its broad and profound inner meaning can only manifest itself to, and be experienced and understood by, practitioners who are at different levels of true cultivation. Only then can one truly see what the Fa is.

Li Hongzhi
February 6, 1995

True Cultivation

My truly cultivating disciples, what I have taught you is the Fa for cultivation of Buddha and Dao. Nonetheless, you pour out your grievances to me over the loss of your worldly interests, rather than feeling upset for being unable to let go of ordinary human attachments. Is this cultivation? Whether you can let go of ordinary

---

[5] Falun Dafa (fah-lun dah-fah)— "The Great (Cultivation) Way of the Law Wheel."

human attachments is a fatal test on your way to becoming a truly extraordinary being. Every disciple who truly cultivates must pass it, for it is the dividing line between a practitioner and an everyday person.

As a matter of fact, when you panic over infringements upon your reputation, self-interests, and feelings among everyday people, it already indicates that you can't let go of ordinary human attachments. You must remember this: Cultivation itself is not painful—the key lies in your inability to let go of ordinary human attachments. Only when you are about to let go of your reputation, interests, and feelings will you feel pain.

You fell here from a holy, pure, and incomparably splendid world because you had developed attachments at that level. After falling into a world that is, in comparison, most filthy, instead of cultivating yourself to go back in a hurry, you don't let go of those filthy things that you cling to in this filthy world, and you even panic over a little bit of loss. Did you know that in order to save you the Buddha once begged for food among everyday people? Today, I once again make the door wide open and teach this Dafa[6] to save you. I have never felt bitter for the numerous hardships I have suffered. Then what do you have that still cannot be abandoned? Can you bring to a heaven the things deep down inside that you can't let go of?

Li Hongzhi
May 22, 1995

---

[6] Dafa (dah-fah)—"Great Way," short for Falun Dafa.

6

Be Clear Minded

I have told some practitioners that extreme thoughts are caused by thought-karma, but many practitioners now consider all their bad thoughts in everyday life to be thought-karma. This is incorrect. What is there for you to cultivate if you no longer have any bad thoughts?! If you are so pure, aren't you already a Buddha? This understanding is wrong. Only when your mind violently reflects filthy thoughts, or curses Teacher,[7] Dafa, other people, etc., and you cannot get rid of them or suppress them, is it thought-karma. But there is also some weak thought-karma, though it is different from regular thoughts or ideas. You must be clear about this.

Li Hongzhi
May 23, 1995

Enlightenment

In the muddy human world, pearls and fish eyes are jumbled together. A Tathagata must descend to the world quietly. When he teaches the Fa, evil practices are bound to interfere. The Dao and the demonic ways are taught at the same time and in the same world. Amidst truth and falsehood, enlightening is important. How to distinguish them? There are bound to be exceptional people. Those who really have predestined relationships and can be enlightened will come one after another, entering the Dao and obtaining the Fa. They will distinguish the righteous from the evil, obtain true teachings, lighten their bodies, enhance their wisdom,

---

[7] Teacher (or "Master")—a respectful title of address used in China. Here it refers to Teacher Li.

enrich their hearts, and board the boat of the Fa, sailing smoothly. How wonderful! Strive forward with every effort until Consummation.

Those who survive the world without direction and with poor enlightenment quality live for money and die for power, being joyful or anxious over petty gains. They compete bitterly against each other, thus accruing karma throughout their lives. When such people hear the Fa, they laugh at it and spit from their mouths the word "superstition," as they are bound to find it hard to understand and hard to believe deep down inside. These people are the inferior persons who are difficult to save. Their karma is so much that it has enveloped their bodies and sealed off their wisdom; their original nature is gone.

Li Hongzhi
June 14, 1995

Why One Cannot See

Seeing is believing, and what is not seen is disbelieved. This is the view of an inferior person. Humans are lost in illusion and have created a lot of karma, thereby obscuring their original nature: So how could they see? Enlightening comes before seeing. Cultivate your heart and eliminate your karma. Once your original nature comes forth you will be able to see. Yet, with or without seeing, an exceptional person can depend on his enlightening to reach Consummation. People may or may not see, and this is determined by their levels and their inborn quality. A practitioner usually does not see because he is in pursuit of seeing—this is an attachment. Thus, until it is given up he will not see. This is mostly due to the obstacles from karma, an unsuitable environment, or one's cultivation way. There are a multitude of reasons, varying from person to person. Even a person who is able to see may not see clearly, for only seeing unclearly can one enlighten to the Dao. When a person can see everything clearly as if he were personally on the scene, he has achieved the Unlocking of Gong (*kaigong*) and cannot practice cultivation any further since there is nothing for him to enlighten to.

Li Hongzhi
June 16, 1995

Learning the Fa

When learning Dafa, intellectuals should be aware of a most prominent problem: They study Dafa in the same way that everyday people study theoretical writings,[8] such as selecting relevant quotations from renowned people to examine their own conduct. This will hinder a practitioner's progress. Furthermore, upon learning that Dafa has profound, inner meaning and high-level things that can guide cultivation practice at different levels, some people even attempt to examine it word by word, but find nothing in the end. These habits, acquired from studying political theories over a long period of time, are also factors that interfere with cultivation practice; they lead to a misunderstanding of the Fa.

---

[8] theoretical writings—this refers to the theorertical writings of Marxism, Leninism, Maoism, etc.

While learning the Fa, you should not search for relevant parts, stubbornly intending to solve a particular problem. In fact, this is (with the exception of those problems that need an immediate solution) also a form of attachment. The only way to gain a good understanding of Dafa is to study it without any intention. Each time you finish reading *Zhuan Falun,*[9] you have made progress as long as you have gained some understanding. Even if you understood only one point after reading it, you have truly made progress.

Actually, in cultivation practice you ascend by improving yourself gradually and unknowingly. Keep in mind: One should gain things naturally without pursuing them.

Li Hongzhi
September 9, 1995

How to Provide Assistance

Many assistants in different regions have a very high-level understanding of Dafa. They are able to set a good example with their conduct and do a good job organizing their practice groups. Yet there are also some assistants who have not done so well, and this mainly manifests in their methods of work. For instance, in order to make the practitioners listen to them and to make it easier to carry out their work, some assistants have done their work by issuing orders—this is not permitted. Learning the Fa should be

---

[9] *Zhuan Falun* (jwahn fah-lun)—"Turning the Law Wheel"; the main book of Falun Dafa cultivation.

voluntary. If a practitioner does not want to do so from the bottom of his heart, no problem can be solved. Instead, tensions may arise. Tensions will intensify if this isn't corrected, thus severely undermining people's learning the Fa.

Even more serious, some assistants, in order to make practitioners believe and obey them, often circulate some hearsay or something sensational to increase their prestige, or they do unique things to show off. All of these are not allowed. Our assistants serve others on a voluntary basis; they are not the master, nor should they have these attachments.

Then how can you do the assistant job well? First off, you should treat yourself as one of the practitioners instead of considering yourself above them. If there is something that you do not know in your work, you should humbly discuss it with others. If you have done something wrong, you should sincerely tell the practitioners, "I, too, am a practitioner just as you are, so it's inevitable that I'll make mistakes in my work. Now that I've made a mistake, let's do what's right." If you sincerely want to have all practitioners collaborate to get things done, what results will you get? No one will say that you are good for nothing. Instead, they will think that you have learned the Fa well and are open-minded. In fact, Dafa is here, and everyone is studying it. Practitioners will measure every move an assistant makes according to Dafa, and whether it is good or not can be clearly distinguished. Once you have the intention of building yourself up, the practitioners will think that you have a *xinxing*[10] problem. Therefore, only by being modest can you do

---

[10] *xinxing* (shin-shing)—"mind nature" or "heart nature"; "moral character."

11

things well. Your reputation is established based on a good understanding of the Fa. How could a practitioner be free of mistakes?

Li Hongzhi
September 10, 1995

Firmament

The vastness of the universe and the enormity of the celestial bodies can never be understood by man through exploration; the minuteness of matter can never be detected by man. The human body is so mysterious that it is beyond man's knowledge, which can merely scratch the surface. Life is so abundant and complex that it will forever remain an eternal enigma to mankind.

Li Hongzhi
September 24, 1995

Realms

A wicked person is born of jealousy. Out of selfishness and anger he complains about unfairness toward himself.

A benevolent person always has a heart of compassion. With no discontentment or hatred, he takes hardship as joy.

An enlightened being has no attachments at all. He quietly observes the everyday people blinded by delusion.

Li Hongzhi
September 25, 1995

What is Emptiness?

What is emptiness? Being free of attachments is the true state of emptiness. It does not mean being empty of matter. Zen Buddhism has reached the end of its Dharma,[11] however, and has nothing to teach. In this chaotic Dharma-Ending Period,[12] some scholars still stubbornly hold on to its theory of emptiness, acting irrational and absurd, as though they are enlightened to the fundamentals of its philosophy. Its founder, Boddhidharma, himself acknowledged that his Dharma could only be effective for six generations, and that afterwards there would be nothing to pass down. Why not awaken to it? If one says that everything is empty, with no Fa, no Buddha, no image, no self, and no existence, what thing is Boddhidharma? If there is no Dharma, what thing is Zen Buddhism's theory of emptiness? If there is no Buddha, no image, who is Sakyamuni?[13] If there is no name, no image, no self, no existence, and everything

---

[11] Dharma—this term is the conventional translation for the Chinese word "Fa" in the context of Buddhism.

[12] Dharma-Ending Period—according to Buddha Sakyamuni, the Dharma-Ending Period was to begin five hundred years after his death, at which point his Dharma would no longer be able to save people.

[13] Sakyamuni—Buddha Sakyamuni, or "the Buddha," Siddhartha Gautama. Popularly known as the founder of Buddhism, he is said to have lived in ancient India around the 5th century B.C.

is empty, why do you bother to eat and drink? Why do you wear clothes? What if your eyes were dug out? Why are you so attached to the seven emotions and six desires of an everyday person? Actually, what a Tathagata means by "emptiness" is being free from every ordinary human attachment. Non-omission is the true essence of emptiness. To begin with, the universe exists because of matter and is composed of and remains as matter. How could it be empty? It is not that the teaching of a Tathagata is bound to be short lived and the principles will cease to exist–the teaching of an Arhat is not the Buddha's teaching. Enlighten to it! Enlighten to it!

Li Hongzhi
September 28, 1995

Determination

With Teacher here, you are full of confidence. Without Teacher here, you lose your interest in cultivation. It appears as though you cultivate yourself for Teacher and have come here out of short-lived interest. This is a major weakness of an average person. Sakyamuni, Jesus, Lao Zi,[14] and Confucius have been gone for over two thousand years, yet their disciples have never felt that they couldn't practice cultivation without their masters around. Cultivation is your own affair, and nobody else can do it for you. The teacher can only, on the surface, tell you the laws and principles. It is your own responsibility to cultivate your heart, let go of your desires, attain wisdom, and eliminate confusion. If you have come here out of short-lived interest, your mind will certainly be undetermined. You are bound

[14] Lao Zi (laow dzz)—known as the author of the *Dao De Jing*, he is regarded as the founder of Daoism and thought to have lived sometime around the 4th century B.C.

to forget the fundamentals while living in human society. If you don't firmly hold to your faith, you will gain nothing in this life. No one knows when there will be another chance. It's very hard!

Li Hongzhi
October 6, 1995

The Teachings in Buddhism are the Weakest and Tiniest Portion of the Buddha Fa

All sentient beings! Never use Buddhism to measure the Dafa of Zhen-Shan-Ren, because it is immeasurable. People have already become accustomed to calling the scriptures of Buddhism the Fa. In fact, the cosmic bodies are so vast that they are beyond a Buddha's understanding of the universe. The Taiji[15] theory of the Dao School is also a low-level understanding of the universe. At the level of ordinary humans there is no actual Fa, except for a tiny smattering of phenomena on the boundary of the universe that can enable one to practice cultivation. Since everyday people are beings at the lowest level, they are not allowed to know the real Buddha Fa. But people have heard sages say: "Worshipping Buddha can plant causal seeds for the opportunity to practice cultivation; cultivators who chant incantations can receive protection from higher beings; observing precepts can enable one to reach a cultivator's standard." Throughout history, people have been studying whether what the Enlightened One taught is the Buddha Fa. The Tathagata's teaching is the manifestation of Buddha-nature, and it can also be called a manifestation of Fa. But it is not the universe's actual Fa, because in

---

[15] Taiji (tye-jee)—"Great Ultimate"; the Taiji is the symbol of the Dao School, and what is popularly referred to in the West as the "yin-yang" symbol.

the past people were absolutely prohibited from knowing the Buddha Fa's true manifestation. The Buddha Fa could only be enlightened to by someone who had reached a high level through cultivation practice, so it was even more the case that people were not allowed to know the true essence of cultivation practice. Falun Dafa has for the first time throughout the ages left the nature of the universe—the Buddha Fa—to human beings; this amounts to leaving them a ladder to ascend to heaven. So how could you measure the Dafa of the universe with what was once taught in Buddhism?

Li Hongzhi
October 8, 1995

What is Wisdom?

People think that the renowned persons, scholars and different sorts of experts in human society are great. In fact, they are all really insignificant, for they are everyday people. Their knowledge is only that tiny bit understood by the modern science of human society. In the vast universe, from the most macroscopic to the most microscopic, human society is exactly in the very middle, in the outermost layer, and on the outermost surface. Also, its living beings are the lowest form of existence, so their understanding of matter and mind is very limited, superficial, and pitiful. Even if someone were to grasp all of mankind's knowledge, he would still remain an everyday person.

Li Hongzhi
October 9, 1995

It is not a Job, but Cultivation Practice

Whether you can follow the requirements I have set for assistance centers is a very important matter of principle, and affects the way the Fa spreads in the future. Why can't you let go of the routines that you've developed over a long period of time in bureaucratic offices? Do not treat assistance centers as administrative offices in human society and adopt their methods and approaches, such as issuing documents, launching policy implementations, or "uplifting the people's understanding." A Dafa cultivator should only improve his *xinxing* in cultivation, and raise his Attainment Status and level. Sometimes even a meeting is held in the format of the everyday people's workplace. For example, it will have some kind of official make a speech or have a certain leader give a summary. Nowadays, even the state is trying to reform those corrupt practices and bureaucratic procedures in society. As a practitioner, you already know that every aspect of mankind is no longer good in the Dharma-Ending Period. Why can't you let go of those work methods that are the least suitable for cultivation practice? We absolutely will never turn it into an administrative institution or an enterprise in society.

Before, some retired people with nothing to do found Falun Dafa good and offered to help so as to fill an aching void in their leisurely lives. Of course that won't do! Falun Dafa is for cultivation practice—it is not a job. All of our volunteer workers must first be genuine practitioners with high-level *xinxing*, as they are role models for *xinxing* cultivation. We do not need the types of leaders like those among everyday people.

Li Hongzhi
October 12, 1995

Practicing Cultivation After Retirement

It is a great pity that some practitioners who attended my lectures and have good inborn quality have stopped practicing because they are busy with work. If they were average, everyday people, I would say nothing more and leave them alone. But these people still have some promise. Human morality is declining a thousand miles a day, and everyday people are all drifting along with the current. The farther away from the Dao, the more difficult to return through cultivation. As a matter of fact, cultivation practice is about cultivating one's heart and mind. The complex environment of the workplace, in particular, provides a good opportunity for you to improve your *xinxing*. Once retired, won't you lose the best environment for practicing cultivation? What will you cultivate without any troubles? How can you improve yourself? One's lifetime is limited. Oftentimes you plan things quite well, but do you know whether you will have sufficient time left for your cultivation? Cultivation practice is not child's play. It is more serious than anything of everyday people—it isn't something to take for granted. Once you miss the opportunity, when will you be able to get a human body again in the sixfold path of reincarnation? Opportunity knocks but once. Once the illusion that you cannot let go of disappears, you will realize what you have lost.

Li Hongzhi
October 13, 1995

When the Fa is Right

When man does not have virtue, natural calamities and man-made disasters will abound. When the earth does not have virtue, everything will wither and fall. When heaven deviates from the Dao, the ground will crack, the sky will collapse, and all the universe will be empty. When the Fa is right, the universe will be right. Life will flourish, heaven and earth will be stable, and the Fa will exist forever.

Li Hongzhi
November 12, 1995

Sage

He is on a Providential mission in this world as well as in heaven above. He possesses mighty virtue while maintaining a benevolent heart, he carries great aspirations while minding minor details. With broad knowledge of laws and principles, he is able to unravel uncertainties. By benefiting society and saving people, he builds up his merit naturally.

Li Hongzhi
November 17, 1995

Seeking Discipleship with Teacher

Dafa is being spread far and wide. Those who hear about it are looking for it. Those who have obtained it are delighted with it. The number of cultivators is increasing daily and becoming countless. Nonetheless, most of the self-learners have the intention of formally seeking discipleship with Teacher, for they are concerned that they might not have received the genuine teachings if they have not seen Teacher in person. This is actually due to a shallow understanding of the Fa. My teaching Dafa widely is to offer salvation to all. Whoever learns it is my disciple. Not following old rituals and conventions, I ignore superficial formalities and only look at one's heart. If you do not genuinely cultivate yourself, what's the use of formally acknowledging me as "Teacher"? A person who truly cultivates will gain things naturally without pursuing them. All of the gong[16] and Fa lie in the book, and one will naturally obtain them by reading Dafa. Those who learn it will change automatically, and they will already be in the Dao by reading the book over and over again. Teacher will certainly have Law Bodies (*fashen*) safeguarding them quietly. With perseverance, they are bound to attain the Righteous Attainment in the future.

Li Hongzhi
December 8, 1995

An Explicit Reminder

---

[16] *gong* (gong)—"cultivation energy."

20

At present there is a prominent problem: When some practitioners' Primordial Spirits (*yuanshen*) leave their bodies, they see or come into contact with certain dimensions at certain levels. Feeling that it is so wonderful and that everything there truly exists, they don't want to return. This has resulted in the death of their flesh bodies. So they stayed in that realm and could not come back. Yet none of them had reached beyond the Three Realms. I have addressed this problem before. Do not get attached to any dimension in your cultivation. Only when you have completed the entire course of cultivation can you achieve Consummation. So when your Primordial Spirit goes out, no matter how wonderful you find those places, you must return.

We also have some practitioners with a misunderstanding. They think that once they practice Falun Dafa they are assured that their physical bodies will never die. Our cultivation system does cultivate both mind and body; a practitioner can prolong his life while he practices cultivation. But some people have not diligently made progress in their In-Triple-World-Law cultivation, and they always linger at a certain level. After much effort to move up to another level, they then linger at that level again. Cultivation is serious, so it is difficult to guarantee that one's life will not come to an end at the predestined time. Yet this problem does not exist for Beyond-Triple-World-Law cultivation practice. But the situation with In-Triple-World-Law is more complicated.

Li Hongzhi
December 21, 1995

For Whom do You Practice Cultivation?

21

When some people resort to the media to criticize *qigong*, some practitioners waver in determination and give up their practice; it's as if those who take advantage of the media are wiser than Buddha Fa, and that some practitioners cultivate for others. There are also people who become scared in the face of pressure and give up their cultivation. Can these kinds of people achieve the Righteous Attainment? At the crucial moment, won't they even betray Buddha? Isn't fear an attachment? Cultivation practice is like great waves sifting the sand: What remains is gold.

As a matter of fact, from ancient times to the present, human society has had a principle called mutual-generation and mutual-inhibition. So where there is good, there is bad; where there is right, there is evil; where there is compassion, there is wickedness; where there are humans, there are ghosts; where there are Buddhas, there are demons. It is even more present in human society. Where there is positive, there is negative; where there is advocacy, there is opposition; where there are those who believe, there are those who disbelieve; where there are good people, there are bad ones; where there are selfless people, there are selfish ones; and where there are people who can make sacrifices for others, there are people who will stop at nothing to benefit themselves. This was a principle in the past. Therefore, if an individual, a group, or even a nation wants to accomplish something good, there will be an equal amount of negative resistance. After success, one will thus feel that it was hard won and should be treasured. This is how mankind has developed (the principle of mutual-generation and mutual-inhibition will change in the future).

To put it another way, cultivation practice is supernormal. No matter who a person is, isn't his criticism of *qigong* from an ordinary human perspective? Does he have any right to deny the Buddha Fa and cultivation? Can any of mankind's organizations rise above Gods and Buddhas? Do those who criticize *qigong* have the capacity to command Buddhas? Will Buddhas be bad simply because he says so? Will Buddhas cease to exist simply because he claims that there are no Buddhas? The Dharma's tribulation during the "Great Cultural Revolution" resulted from the evolution of cosmic phenomena. Buddhas, Daos and Gods all follow heaven's will. The Dharma's tribulation was a tribulation for humans and religions, rather than a tribulation for Buddhas.

The greatest reason for religions being undermined is the degeneration of the human mind. People worship Buddha not to cultivate Buddhahood, but to seek Buddha's blessings so that they can make a fortune, eliminate adversity, have a son, or lead a comfortable life. Everyone accrued a lot of karma in previous lives. How could one live comfortably? How could a person not pay for his karma after doing bad deeds? Seeing the human mind not right, demons have come out of their caves one after another to bring trouble and chaos to the human world. Upon seeing the human mind not right, Gods and Buddhas left their posts and abandoned the temples one after another. Many foxes, weasels, ghosts, and snakes have been brought into the temples by those who come to pray for wealth and profit. How could such temples not be in trouble? Human beings are sinners. Buddhas do not punish people, because all people are driven by ignorance and have already done harm to themselves. Moreover, they have accrued great amounts of karma for themselves, and great catastrophes soon await them. Would there still be any need to punish them? In fact, if a person does something wrong, he is bound to suffer retribution sometime in the future. It is just that people do not realize or believe it; they regard mishaps as accidents.

Regardless of who or what social forces tell you not to practice cultivation anymore, you then give up your cultivation. Do you practice cultivation for them? Will they give you the Righteous Attainment? Isn't your inclination toward them blind faith? This, in fact, is true ignorance. Besides, we aren't a *qigong* practice, but Buddha Fa cultivation practice. Isn't any form of pressure a test to see whether your faith in the Buddha Fa is fundamentally strong? If you still are not fundamentally resolute in the Fa, everything else is out of question.

Li Hongzhi
December 21, 1995

The Buddha Fa's Terminology

Some practitioners once were lay Buddhists and have a very deep impression of the terms in Buddhist scriptures. When they find that I use words identical to those in Buddhism, they consider them to have the same meanings as in Buddhism. In fact, they do not denote exactly the same meanings. Some terms in the Buddhism of the Han region are Chinese vocabulary, and they are not exclusively terms from Buddhism.

The key point is that these practitioners still cannot let go of the things in Buddhism, for they do not realize that their impressions from Buddhism still affect their minds, nor do they have a sufficient understanding of practicing no second cultivation way. Actually, isn't the superficial similarity that one perceives causing interference? If you misinterpret my words, aren't you practicing cultivation in Buddhism?

Li Hongzhi
December 21, 1995

Pacify the External by Cultivating the Internal

If man does not value virtue, the world will be in great chaos and out of control; everyone will become enemies of one another and live without happiness. Living without happiness, they will not fear death. Lao Zi said, "If the populace doesn't fear death, what good will it do to threaten them with death"? This is a great, imminent danger. A peaceful world is what people hope for. If at this point an excessive number of laws and decrees are created to secure stability, the result will only turn out the opposite. In order to solve this problem, virtue has to be cultivated around the world— only this way can the problem be fundamentally resolved. If officials are unselfish, the state will not be corrupt. If the population values self-cultivation and nurturing virtues, and if both administrators and civilians exercise self-restraint in their minds, the whole nation will be stable and supported by the people. Being solid and stable, the nation will automatically intimidate foreign enemies and peace will thus reign under heaven. This is the work of a sage.

Li Hongzhi
January 5, 1996

Further Elimination of Attachments

My disciples! Master[17] is very worried, but this cannot help! Why

25

can't you abandon the ordinary human mindset? Why are you so reluctant to take a step forward? Our practitioners, including our staff, are jealous of each other even in their work for Dafa. Can you become a Buddha like this? I want to have a loose administration simply because you cannot let go of ordinary human things and so will feel uneasy in your work. Dafa belongs to the entire universe, and not to any one, insignificant individual. Whoever does the work is spreading Dafa. It is not important whether it should be done by you or by others. Are you going to bring to a paradise this attachment that you cannot let go of, and contend with Buddhas? Nobody should treat Dafa as his or her own exclusive thing. Eliminate that feeling injustice in your mind! When your mind cannot get over something, isn't it caused by your attachment? Our practitioners should not think that they are above that attachment! I hope that everyone will examine himself, because you are all cultivators, with the exception of me, Li Hongzhi. Everyone should think about it: Why do I teach so great a Fa in the time of Last Havoc?[18] If I disclose the truth, I will be teaching an evil practice since there will definitely be those who learn the Fa because of this. That would be studying the Fa with pursuit. When saving people, the only way for them to eliminate their attachments is by having the right intention. It is known to all that a person won't succeed in cultivation without giving up attachments. Why don't you dare to abandon more and go one step further? In

---

[17] Master—the Chinese term used here, *shifu*, is composed of two characters: one means "teacher," and the other "father." The author often uses this term in a self-referrential manner.

[18] Last Havoc—it is believed in cultivation circles that the universe has three phases of evolution (Beginning Havoc, Middle Havoc, and Last Havoc), and that now is the Last Havoc's final period.

fact, there must be an unspeakable reason for my teaching this Dafa. Once the truth is revealed, it will be too late for regrets. I have seen the attachments in some of you, but I cannot tell you them directly. If I did, you would keep Master's words in mind and become attached to them for the rest of your life. I do not wish to ruin even one of my disciples. Saving people is just so difficult, and having them enlighten is even more difficult. More importantly, everyone should carefully examine himself in this light. You all know that Dafa is good, so why can't you let go of your attachments?

Li Hongzhi

January 6, 1996

Validation

The Buddha Fa can save mankind, but it is not for the salvation of human beings that the Buddha Fa came into existence. The Buddha Fa can unravel the mysteries of the universe, life, and science. It enables mankind to resume the correct path in science, but it is not for the guidance of mankind's science that the Buddha Fa has been brought forth.

The Buddha Fa is the nature of the universe. It is the factor that created the origin of matter, and it is the reason for the genesis of the universe.

In the future there will be many experts and scholars whose wisdom will be broadened through the Buddha Fa. They will become the new mankind's pioneers in different fields of learning. Yet it is not for you to become a pioneer that the Buddha Fa has given you wisdom. You have attained it because you are a cultivator. That is, you are first a cultivator and then an expert. Then, as a cultivator, you should make use of all feasible conditions to spread Dafa and validate Dafa as a correct and a genuine science, rather than preaching or idealism—this is every cultivator's obligation. Without this enormous Buddha Fa there would be nothing, including everything in the universe, from the most macroscopic to the most microscopic, as well as all of human society's knowledge.

Li Hongzhi
January 8, 1996

A Cultivator is Naturally Part of It

For a cultivator, all the frustrations he comes across among everyday people are trials, and all the compliments he receives are tests.

Li Hongzhi
January 14, 1996

What is Forbearance (*Ren*)?

Forbearance is the key to improving one's *xinxing*. To endure with anger, grievance, or tears is the forbearance of an everyday person who is attached to his concerns. To endure completely without anger or grievance is the forbearance of a cultivator.

Li Hongzhi
January 21, 1996

What is Mi Xin?[19]

Chinese people today really turn pale at the mere mention of the two characters "*mi xin*," because many people call everything that they don't believe *mi xin*. In fact, these two characters, *mi xin*, were coated with an ultra "leftist" garb during the Great Cultural Revolution, and they were used at that time as the most damaging term against the national culture. Being the most horrifying label, it has become the most irresponsible pet phrase of those simple-minded and stubborn people. Even those self-proclaimed, so-called "materialists" label everything beyond their knowledge or beyond the understanding of science as *mi xin*. If things were to have been understood according to that theory, mankind would not have made any advancements. Neither would science have developed further, because all of science's new progressions and discoveries have been beyond the understanding of its predecessors. Then aren't these people themselves practicing idealism? Once a human being believes in something, isn't that, itself a fixation? Isn't it true that some people's trust in modern science or modern medicine is also *mi xin*? Isn't it true that people's revering their idols is *mi xin* as well? Actually, the two characters *mi* and *xin* form a very common term. Once people zealously believe in something—including the truth—it becomes *mi xin*; it doesn't denote

---

[19] *mi xin* (mee shin)—"superstition," or "blind faith."

29

any derogatory meaning. It is only that when those with ulterior motives launch their attacks on others that "*mi xin*" gets coated with the connotation of feudalism,[20] and so it has become a misleading and combatative term that can further incite simple-minded people to echo it.

As a matter of fact, the two characters, *mi xin*, themselves should not be used this way, nor should the imposed connotation exist. What the two characters *mi* and *xin* imply is not something negative. Without *mi xin* in discipline, soldiers would not have combatative abilities; without *mi xin* in their schools and teachers, students would not acquire knowledge; without *mi xin* in their parents, children would not be brought up well-mannered; without *mi xin* in their careers, people would not do a good job in their work. Without beliefs, human beings would have no moral standards; the human mind would not have good thoughts, and it would be overcome by evil thoughts. The moral values of the human society at that time would decline rapidly. Possessed by evil thoughts, everyone would become enemies of one another and would stop at nothing to satisfy their selfish desires. Although those bad people who have imposed negative connotations on the two characters of *mi* and *xin* have achieved their objectives, they have very likely ruined mankind in terms of its original nature.

Li Hongzhi
January 22, 1996
Revised on August 29, 1996

Sickness Karma

---

[20] "feudalism"—in contemporary Mainland China, this is a very negative term that connotes backwardness and superstition.

Why does a new practitioner who has just begun studying the practice, or a veteran practitioner whose body has been adjusted, experience physical discomfort in his cultivation, as though he were seriously ill? And why does this happen once in a while? When I was teaching the Fa, I told you that this is to eliminate your karma and to improve your enlightenment quality while eliminating the karma from your different previous lives. Besides, this is also to test whether you are determined in following Dafa; this will continue until your cultivation reaches Beyond-Triple-World-Law. This is putting it in general terms.

As a matter of fact, a person does not know how many lifetimes—in each of which he has accrued a great deal of karma—he has gone through. When a person reincarnates after death, some of his sickness-karma is pressed into his body at the microscopic level. When he reincarnates, the new physical body's matter has no sickness-karma on the surface (but there are exceptions for those with too much karma). What was pressed into the body in the previous life then comes out, and when it returns to the surface of this physical body, the person will become ill. Yet the sickness will usually appear to be triggered by an external condition in the physical world. This way it will superficially conform to the objective laws of our physical world. That is, it will comply with this human world's principles. As a result, everyday people have no way of knowing the actual truth about the cause of the sickness, and they are thus lost in delusion without being enlightened. Once ill, the person will take medicine or seek various kinds of treatments, which in effect press the sickness back into the body again. Consequently, instead of paying for the sickness-karma from his wrongdoing in the previous life, he will do some additional bad things in this life to hurt others; this will bring about new sickness-karma and lead to different kinds of sicknesses. Nevertheless, he will again take medicine or use various treatments to press the sickness back into the body. Surgery can only remove flesh in the superficial physical dimension, while the sickness-karma in another dimension has not been touched at all—it is simply beyond the reach of modern medical technology. When the sickness recurs, the person will again seek treatment. When a person reincarnates after death, any sickness-karma that has accrued will again be pressed back into his body. This cycle goes on one lifetime after another; it is unknown how much sickness-karma accumulates in a person's body. This is why I have said that all of today's mankind has come to this point with karma rolling on top of karma; besides sickness-karma, a person has other kinds of karma as well. Therefore, people have hardships, tribulations, and tensions in their lives. How could they only pursue happiness without paying for karma? People nowadays have so much karma that they are soaked in it, and they will encounter unpleasant things at any time and in any situation. Whenever a person leaves his home, there will be something bad awaiting him. When there are disagreements, however, people do not endure them and fail to realize that they are paying off their karma from the past. If a person is not treated well by others, he will treat others even worse, thereby producing new karma before paying for the old. This makes society's moral values decline daily, and everyone becomes enemies among one another. Many people cannot think through this: What's happened to people today? What's going on with today's society? If mankind continues like this it will be extremely dangerous!

As a cultivator, in addition to the karma eliminated by Master, you have to pay for a portion yourself. You will thus feel physically uncomfortable, as if you were suffering from sickness. Cultivation practice is to cleanse you from your life's origin. The human body is like the annual rings of a tree, whereby each ring contains sickness-karma. So your body must be cleansed from the very center. Were karma to be pushed out all at once, however, you would not be able to take it, as it would endanger your life. Only a piece or two can be pushed out every once in a while, allowing you to overcome it and pay for your karma through suffering. But this is only that little bit left for you yourself to endure after I have eliminated karma for you. This will continue until your cultivation reaches the highest form of In-Triple-World-Law (i.e., the Pure-White Body), when all your karma will have been pushed out. Yet there are also some people with very little sickness-karma, and there are other special cases. Cultivation practice in Beyond-Triple-World-Law is that of the purest Arhat body—a body that does not have any sickness-karma. But as for a person that has not yet achieved Consummation and who is still practicing cultivation toward higher levels of Beyond-Triple-World-Law, he will still suffer and have tribulations and trials to advance his level. These will only involve interpersonal tensions or other things in the area of *xinxing* and the further abandonment of his attachments; he will no longer have physical sickness-karma.

Sickness-karma isn't something that can be casually eliminated for an everyday person; this is absolutely impossible for a non-practitioner, who must rely on medical treatment. Doing this at will for an everyday person would actually be undermining the principles of heaven, for it would mean that a person can do bad things without having to pay for the karma. It is absolutely unacceptable for a person to not repay his debts—the principles of heaven won't permit it! Even the treatments of ordinary *qigong* also push karma to the inside of a person's body. When a person has too much karma and is still doing bad things, he will face destruction—the complete destruction of both body and soul—at his death, which is total extinction. When treating a sickness for a human being, a great enlightened being can completely eliminate the karmic cause of that sickness, but this is done mainly with the purpose of saving people.

Li Hongzhi

March 10, 1996

Cultivators' Avoidances

Those who are attached to their reputations practice an evil way, full of intention. Once they gain renown in this world, they are bound to say good but mean evil, thereby misleading the public and undermining the Fa.

Those who are attached to money seek wealth and feign their cultivation. Undermining the practice and the Fa, they waste their lifetimes instead of cultivating Buddhahood.

Those who are attached to lust are no different from wicked people. While reciting the scriptures, they even cast furtive glances; they are far from the Dao and are wicked, everyday people.

Those who are attached to affection for family will definitely be burned, entangled, and tormented by it. Pulled by the threads of affection and plagued by them throughout their lives, they will find it too late to regret at the end of their lives.

Li Hongzhi
April 15, 1996

Perfect Harmony

(I.)
People in various workplace environments are involved in different aspects of killing. The balancing of lives manifests in different ways. As a cultivator, you should first of all let go of every attachment and conform to the ways of human society, as this is maintaining the Fa's manifestation at a certain level. If no one performed the human jobs, the Fa at this level would cease to exist.

(II.)
Lives within the Fa exist or die naturally. The universe goes through formation, settlement, and degeneration, and human beings undergo birth, aging, illness, and death. There also exist unnatural births and deaths in the balancing of lives. There is sacrifice in forbearance, and a complete sacrifice is a higher principle of non-omission.

Li Hongzhi
April 19, 1996

Non-Omission

There is sacrifice in forbearance. Being able to make sacrifices is the result of improving in one's cultivation. The Fa has different levels. A cultivator's understanding of the Fa is his understanding of the Fa at his cultivation level. Different cultivators understand the Fa differently because they are at different levels.

For cultivators at different levels, the Fa has different requirements. Sacrifice is evidenced by one's being detached from ordinary human attachments. If a person can indeed calmly abandon everything with his heart being unaffected, he is actually at that level already. Yet cultivation practice is to improve yourself: You are already able to abandon the attachment, so why not also abandon the fear of attachment, itself? Isn't abandonment without omission a higher sacrifice? Yet if a cultivator or an everyday person who cannot even make fundamental sacrifices also discusses this principle, he is actually undermining the Fa by making excuses for the attachments he cannot let go of.

Li Hongzhi
April 26, 1996

Cultivation and Work

With the exception of professional cultivators in temples, the vast majority of our Falun Dafa practitioners are practicing cultivation in the society of everyday people. Through studying and practicing Dafa, all of you can take fame and self-interest lightly. Yet, a lack of in-depth understanding of the Fa has given rise to a problem: A small number of disciples have given up their jobs among everyday people or refuse to be promoted to leadership positions. This has incurred much unnecessary interference in their work and lives, directly affecting their cultivation. Some decent business people think that they have taken money lightly and, at the same time, that doing business may harm others and affect their own cultivation. They have also given up their businesses.

In fact, Dafa's content is profound. Abandoning an ordinary human mindset does not mean giving up an everyday person's job. Giving up fame and self-interest is not to distance yourself from the society of everyday people. I have repeatedly pointed out that those who practice cultivation in the society of everyday people must conform to the ways of everyday people's society.

Viewed from another perspective, if all leadership positions in the society of everyday people were filled by people like us who can let go of the concern for their own reputation and self-interest, what great benefits would it bring to people? And what would be brought to society if greedy people were to assume power? If all business people were cultivators of Dafa, what would society's morality be like?

The Dafa of the universe (the Buddha Fa) is coherent and complete, from the highest level to the lowest level. You should know that ordinary human society also comprises a level of the Fa. If everyone were to study Dafa and give up their jobs in society, ordinary human society would cease to exist, and so would this level of the Fa. Ordinary human society is the manifestation of the Fa at the lowest level, and it is also the form of existence of life and matter for the Buddha Fa at this level.

Li Hongzhi
April 26, 1996

Correction

At present, practitioners in different regions take the following, put forward by the Research Society, as the Fa or my words to spread and study:

Read Dafa selectively,
Cultivate your xinxing sincerely,
Practice the exercises arduously… etc.

Actually, they are not my words, nor do they have a deeper meaning—they certainly are not the Fa. What is meant by "selective reading" differs greatly from my requirement in studying the Fa. As a matter of fact, I was very explicit about reading the books in the article, "Studying the Fa," that I wrote on September 9, 1995. Besides, what is meant by "intensive reading" has caused serious interference with "Studying the Fa." From now on you must pay attention to the seriousness of this problem. I have talked about the reason for Buddhism's disappearance in India and its lesson. If no caution is taken in the future, it will be the beginning of the disruption of the Fa. Attention: When a problem arises, do not try to find out who should be held accountable. Instead, you should examine your own conduct. Do not try to look into who wrote them. Take a lesson from it and be careful in the future.

Li Hongzhi
April 28, 1996

Durability

It seems that there still exists a problem if we are to keep Dafa unchanged forever. Namely, there are always practitioners who, driven by their desire to show off and their intention of being different, do things that interfere with Dafa as soon as an opportunity arises. This is sometimes really serious. For example, recently someone has been saying that I individually taught a practitioner the essentials of the exercises (the fact is that I only corrected a practitioner's movements when he asked me). That in effect invalidates the exercise movements I have been teaching in different regions for the past few years. While I am still around and under the circumstance that the instructional videotape is still available, this person even publicly altered Dafa's exercise movements. He told the practitioners not to practice according to the videotape but to follow him, claiming that Teacher has high-level *gong*, is different from his students, and so on. He also told the practitioners to practice according to their own conditions first, to gradually make changes in the future, and so on.

From the very beginning I have taught the exercises in their entirety, for I have been concerned that some practitioners might make arbitrary changes. The energy mechanism can never be changed once it forms. This problem may seem insignificant, but it is actually the beginning of a serious disruption of the Fa. Some people take the transitional movements as individual ones and tell practitioners to do them in a standardized way. Doing that sort of thing is trying to be different. This has brought about very serious effects in different regions at the present time. My disciples! My instructional videotapes are still available—why would you follow these people so readily?! Dafa is the solemn, great Fa of the universe. Even if you disrupt just a bit of it, what a mammoth sin that is! As a cultivator, you should practice cultivation in an open and dignified manner and look at the larger picture. How could it possibly be that everyone's movements are exactly the same, without any slight differences? Don't focus your mind on such trivialities. The exercise movements are a way to help reach Consummation, and they are certainly important. But instead of going down a dead end, you should devote more effort to improving your *xinxing*. In fact, most interference for Dafa comes internally, from practitioners themselves. External factors can only affect a few individuals and are unable to alter the Fa. Whether it be at present or in the future, those who can undermine our Fa are none other than our own practitioners. Be careful! Our Fa is unchangeable and eternal. Under no circumstances and for no reason can anyone alter even a bit of the movements with which we are to reach Consummation. Otherwise, this person is undermining the Fa, regardless of whether his motives are good or not.

Li Hongzhi
May 11, 1996

Don't Make Wild Statements

Recently an expression has been circulating. That is, when practitioners spread Dafa and thereby help some people with predestined relationships to obtain the Fa and begin cultivation practice, some of these practitioners claim that they have saved people. They say, "Today I saved a few people, and you saved several people," and so on. Actually, it is the Fa that saves people, and only Master can do this thing. You merely help people with predestined relationships to obtain the Fa. Whether they can truly be saved still depends on whether they can reach Consummation. Be careful: Making such wild statements—whether intentional or not—will shock even a Buddha. Don't create obstacles for your own cultivation practice. You must also cultivate your speech in this regard. I hope you can understand.

Li Hongzhi
May 21, 1996

Awakening

The time for studying Dafa and doing actual cultivation is limited. Many practitioners have realized that they need to hurry up and diligently make continual progress. Yet some practitioners do not treasure their time, and focus their minds on tangential issues. Since this book of Dafa, *Zhuan Falun*, was published, many people have compared the recordings of my lectures with the book, claiming that the Research Society changed Teacher's words. Some others have said that the book was written with the help of so-and-so, and they have thus undermined Dafa. I am telling you now that Dafa belongs to me, Li Hongzhi. It is taught to save you and spoken from my mouth. Moreover, when I taught the Fa, I did not use any scripts or other materials, but only a piece of paper concerning what I would teach to my students; its contents were quite simple, with only a few points that no one else could understand. Every time I taught the Fa I presented it from a different angle and spoke according to the students' ability to comprehend. So every time I taught the Fa, I would address the same issue from a different angle. Furthermore, this book of Fa represents the nature of the universe and is the true manifestation of the mighty Buddha Fa. It is what I originally had—that which I recalled after attaining Enlightenment through cultivation practice. I then made it public in ordinary human language, and I taught it to you as well as to those in heavens, thereby rectifying the universe with the Fa. To make cultivation convenient for students, I assigned some students to transcribe the contents of my lectures from the tape recordings without changing any of my original words. Then they gave it to me for revision. The students merely copied my revisions or typed them on a computer so that I could make further revisions. As far as *Zhuan Falun* is concerned, I personally revised it three times before it was finalized and published.

No one has ever made even a slight change to the contents of this book of Dafa. What's more, who could possibly do that? There are three reasons for its differences from the tape recordings. First, to help people practice cultivation I combined many of my Fa-lectures when doing the revisions. Secondly, while lecturing on the Fa, I taught according to students' different abilities to comprehend and in keeping with the situations and circumstances at that time; therefore, I had to modify the structure of the language when editing it into a book. Thirdly, when cultivators study it, misunderstandings can occur as a result of differences between the speech and the written language, so modification was needed. Nonetheless, the form and colloquial style of my lectures on the Fa were still preserved. *Zhuan Falun (Volume Two)*, and *Falun Dafa Explication*, were also personally revised by me before they were published. I incorporated thinking at different levels when writing *Zhuan Falun (Volume Two)*, so some people find the writing style different and are puzzled by it. These are not things of ordinary humans to begin with! In fact, *Volume Two* is reserved for future generations to learn the extent of mankind's degeneration today, thereby leaving people a profound historical lesson. *China Falun Gong*, including its revised version, is only a transitional material in the form of *qigong* for people to understand at the beginning.

Disruption of the Fa takes many forms, of which unintentional disruption by disciples themselves is the most difficult to detect. Sakyamuni's Buddhism began its deterioration in just this way and the lesson is profound.

Disciples must remember: All Falun Dafa texts are the Fa that I have taught, and they are personally revised and edited by me. From now on, no one is allowed to take excerpts from the tape recordings of my Fa-lectures, nor compile them into written materials. Regardless of whatever your excuses are, that is still undermining the Fa; this includes the so-called "contrasting the differences between the speech and its written form," and so on.

Nothing in the evolution of the cosmic bodies or in mankind's development is accidental. Human society's development is directed by history and is driven by the cosmic climate. In the future there will be more people around the world learning Dafa. This is not something that can be done by a hot-headed person simply because he wants to. With an event of this magnitude, how could there not be various arrangements in history? Actually, everything that I have done was arranged countless years ago, and this includes who would obtain the Fa—nothing is accidental. But the way these things manifest is in keeping with ordinary humans. As a matter of fact, the things imparted to me by my several masters in this life are also what I intentionally arranged a few lifetimes ago for them to obtain. When the predestined occasion arrived, they were arranged to impart those things back to me so that I could recall my Fa in its entirety. So let me tell you that this book of Fa is not only studied by those at the human level, but also by beings at higher levels. Because an enormous scope of the cosmic body has deviated from the fundamental nature of the universe, it has to be rectified by the Fa. Mankind is rather insignificant in the vast universe. Earth is nothing but a speck of dust in the universe. If human beings want to be valued by higher beings, they too have to practice cultivation and become higher beings!

Li Hongzhi
May 27, 1996

Stability of the Fa

Some problems have occurred in practitioners' cultivation over the past two years. I have been observing the situation of practitioners' cultivation. To correct the rising problems promptly, I often intentionally write some short articles with specific purposes (called "scriptures" by practitioners) to guide practitioners in their cultivation. The purpose is to leave a stable, healthy, and correct way for Dafa cultivation practice. The future generations for thousands of years to come must cultivate according to the way I have personally left them if they are to reach Consummation.

Recently, however, I saw a collection of materials at a practice site in Hong Kong that were passed there from another region; two of the materials were short articles not intended for publication. This was a serious and intentional attempt to harm Dafa! Even transcribing our tape recordings on your own is wrong! I have made it clear in the article "Awakening" that there is no excuse for anybody's transcribing my words into written materials from the tape recordings—doing this is undermining the Fa. Meanwhile, I have repeatedly emphasized that you cannot circulate the private notes that you took during my lectures. Why do you still do that? What frame of mind drove you to write them? Let me tell you that except for the several officially published books of mine and the dated short articles with my signature that are distributed to different regions by the Research Society, everything transcribed without permission is undermining the Fa. Cultivation is your own matter, and it is your own decision what you pursue. Everyday people all have both demon-nature and Buddha-nature. Demon-nature will come into play once a person's mind isn't right. Let me tell you again that an outsider can never undermine the Fa. Only practitioners can undermine the Fa—remember this!

Every step I, Li Hongzhi, take is to establish an unchangeable and unalterable way for the transmission of Dafa in future generations. Such an enormous Fa will not be over after a moment of popularity. There cannot be any slight deviation in the countless years to come. Safeguarding Dafa with your own conduct is forever the responsibility of Dafa disciples, because Dafa belongs to all sentient beings of the universe, and this includes you.

Li Hongzhi
June 11, 1996

Cultivation Practice and Taking Responsibility

The purpose of cultivating diligently and solidly is to reach Consummation as soon as possible. A practitioner is simply one who eliminates the attachments of an everyday person. Disciples, you need to be clear about what you're doing!

To be responsible to Dafa, the assistance centers, general assistance centers in different regions, and the Research Society have the right to replace any assistant or person in charge of a branch. So at times, persons in positions of responsibility may be replaced according to the different situations. Because a person in charge is, first of all, a practitioner who has come here for cultivation practice rather than to be in charge, he should be able to move up and down in his position. Being assigned a position with responsibility is for cultivation practice, yet a person can practice cultivation all the same without holding a position of responsibility. If the person being replaced cannot get over it in his heart, isn't that caused by his attachment? Isn't it a good opportunity for him to get rid of that attachment? Given this, if he still cannot let go of this attachment, this clearly indicates that it is correct to make the replacement. Being attached to a position of responsibility is itself an unjustified motive for practicing cultivation. So let me remind disciples: You won't be able to reach Consummation without letting go of this attachment.

Li Hongzhi
June 12, 1996

Handling Handwritten Copies of Scriptures

More and more people are now learning Dafa, and the number is doubling on a weekly basis. Publishers' book supplies are inadequate, so they cannot meet the demand. The books are thus unavailable in some regions or in the countryside. Some practitioners have asked me what to do with their handwritten copies of Dafa. Let me tell you that for the time being you can give the copies of *Zhuan Falun* or other scriptures that you have handwritten during your study of Dafa to those who go to the rural areas to spread the practice and the Fa; bringing them to farmers can, at the same time, lessen their economic burdens. Therefore, this requires that practitioners' handwritten copies be legible so that farmers with limited education can understand them. Handwritten copies have the same power of Fa as the printed books.

Li Hongzhi
June 26, 1996

The Fa Conference

It is necessary for disciples to share with one another what they have experienced and learned in their cultivation. There is no problem with them helping one another make progress together, so long as they don't have any intention of showing themselves off. Some conferences for sharing cultivation experiences have been held in different regions to facilitate the dissemination of Dafa. These conferences have all been excellent and healthy, both in form and content. But the practitioners' speeches must be approved by the assistance centers to avoid political issues—which have nothing to do with cultivation practice—or issues that set incorrect trends in cultivation practice and in society. Meanwhile, we should avoid practicing superficial boasting—something which derives from everyday people's theoretical studies. Compiling articles, with the intention of showing oneself off, and as if they were submitted documents, and to read them in public is not permitted. No one should use the intention of showing off to compile articles in the style of official reports and then deliver them in some large public speech.

Large conferences for sharing cultivation experiences that are organized by the general assistance centers at the provincial or city level should not be held on a national scale. A national or an international one should be organized by the Research Society, and it should not be held too frequently. Once a year should be good (except for in special cases). Don't turn them into a formality or competition; instead, make it a solemn Fa conference that can truly facilitate the progression of one's cultivation.

Li Hongzhi
June 26, 1996

A Letter to Shijiazhuang[21] Dafa General Assistance Center

Shijiazhuang Dafa General Assistance Center:

I have learned that your conference for sharing cultivation experiences met with obstacles. There are three reasons for this, from which you will certainly learn a lesson. In fact, this incident has directly affected the Dafa activities in Beijing and the entire country, and it will have a certain negative impact on normal Dafa activities later on. I think that you will definitely realize this and do better in the future.

Additionally, let me say a few more words about Jing Zhanyi's seminars. In Jing Zhanyi's case, these were for the validation of Dafa's scientific nature from the perspective of science, thereby letting the scientific and technological community or the academic world come

---

[21] Shijiazhuang (shr-jyah-jwahng)—a city located in Hebei province, not far south of Beijing.

to understand Dafa. He wasn't supposed to give speeches to practitioners, as doing so would not do any good at all and would only cause new practitioners, or disciples without a solid understanding of the Fa, to develop attachments. Those disciples who study the Fa well will, without needing to listen to such speeches, continue their determined cultivation in Dafa all the same.

More importantly, I have taught the Fa for two years, and I have given disciples two years to practice cultivation. Over disciples' two years of actually cultivating, I have not allowed any activities that have nothing to do with actual cultivation to interfere with the orderly, step-by-step process of improvement arranged for practitioners. If the speeches are not given to the scientific and academic communities to validate Dafa's scientific nature, but rather to the cultivating disciples who have limited time, think about it: Could there be a greater interference for practitioners? I don't even see practitioners so that I will avoid disturbing them. Practitioners cannot calm down for at least a few days after seeing me, and this disrupts the arrangements I had my Law Bodies make for them. I have told the Research Society about this problem, but perhaps it was not made clear to Jing Zhanyi. Now that the matter is over, none of you should try to determine who should be held accountable. I think that the main reason this happened is that you did not realize it. But you must pay attention from now on. Everything we do today is to lay a foundation for the transmission of Dafa over countless years to come, and to leave a perfect, correct, error-free form of cultivation practice. Today I point this out not to criticize anyone, but to correct the form of cultivation practice and leave it for future generations.

Distribute this letter to the assistance centers in different regions.

Li Hongzhi
June 26, 1996

Rectification of One's Character

As Dafa is being cultivated more deeply, many disciples have successively attained Enlightenment or achieved Gradual Enlightenment. They can see the actual, splendid, magnificent scenes in other dimensions. The disciples experiencing the Enlightenment process are so excited that they call my Law Bodies the "second master," or take my Law Bodies as a true and independent master—this is a misunderstanding. Law Bodies are the manifest image of my omnipresent wisdom, but not an independent living being. Some other disciples call the Falun[22] "Master Falun." This is absolutely, grossly wrong. The Falun is another manifest form of my Fa power's nature and Dafa's wisdom—things too wonderful to describe in words. The Falun is the manifestation of the nature of the Fa of all matter in the universe, from the macroscopic level to the microscopic level, and it is not an independent living being.

When you see my Law Bodies and Falun doing those great, miraculous, and magnificent things for you, you disciples must

---

[22] Falun (fah-lun)—"Law Wheel" (see color page at front).

remember not to view or compliment my Law Bodies or Falun with ordinary human thinking. That kind of thinking is a mixed expression of inferior enlightenment quality and inferior *xinxing*. As a matter of fact, all forms that manifest are the concrete manifestations of my using the enormous power of Fa to rectify the Fa and save people.

Li Hongzhi
July 2, 1996

A Brief Explanation of Shan [23]

Shan is the manifestation of the nature of the universe at different levels and in different dimensions. It is also the fundamental nature of the great enlightened beings. Therefore, a cultivator must cultivate Shan and assimilate to the nature of the universe, Zhen-Shan-Ren.[24] The vast cosmic body was born of the universe's nature, Zhen-Shan-Ren. Dafa's being taught in public demonstrates again the original nature of the universe's living beings. Dafa is in perfect harmony: If one separates the three characters of "Zhen-Shan-Ren," each still fully contains Zhen-Shan-Ren. This is because matter is composed of microscopic matter, which is in turn made up of even more microscopic matter—this goes on and on until the end. Therefore, Zhen consists of Zhen-Shan-Ren, Shan consists of Zhen-Shan-Ren, and Ren also consists of Zhen-Shan-

---

[23] Shan (shahn)—"Compassion," "Benevolence," "Kindness," or "Goodness."

[24] Zhen-Shan-Ren (juhn-shahn-ren)—Zhen means "Truth, or Truthfulness"; Shan, "Benevolence, Compassion, or Kindness"; Ren, "Forbearance, Tolerance, Endurance, or Self-Control."

Ren. Isn't the Dao School's cultivating Zhen the cultivation of Zhen-Shan-Ren? Isn't the Buddha School's cultivating Shan also the cultivation of Zhen-Shan-Ren? In fact, they only differ in their superficial forms.

With regard to Shan alone, when it manifests in human society some everyday people who are attached to everyday people's society might raise an ordinary human social question: "If everyone learned Dafa and practiced Shan, how would we handle foreign invasions or wars against us?" In fact, I have already said in *Zhuan Falun* that human society's development is driven by the evolution of the cosmic climate. Are mankind's wars accidental, then? A region with a lot of karma or a region where the human heart has become corrupt is bound to be unstable. If a nationality is to be truly virtuous, it must have little karma; it is certain there will be no wars against it. This is because the principles of Dafa prohibit it, as the nature of the universe governs everything. One doesn't need to worry that a virtuous nation will be invaded. The nature of the universe—Dafa—is present everywhere and encompasses the entire cosmic body, from the macroscopic level to the microscopic level. The Dafa I teach today is not only taught to Eastern people, but also to Westerners at the same time. Their people with good nature should also be saved. All nationalities that should enter the next, new historical era will obtain the Fa and improve as a whole. It is not just a matter of one nationality. Mankind's moral standard will also return to that of original human nature.

Li Hongzhi
July 20, 1996

Annotation on "Rectification of One's Character"

After I said that "Law Bodies and Falun are not independent living beings," some practitioners asked whether this contradicts what *Zhuan Falun* states: "Law Bodies' consciousness and thoughts are controlled by the person. Yet Law Bodies themselves are also complete, independent, and actual individual beings." I think this is due to a poor understanding of the Fa. Law Bodies cannot be understood as the same concept as completely independent lives, because Law Bodies are the willed manifestations of the power and wisdom of the master person's image and thoughts; they are able to accomplishing anything on their own, according to the master person's will. So the practitioners noticed only the second sentence and overlooked the first one: "Law Bodies' consciousness and thoughts are controlled by the master being." Law Bodies thus have not only the independent and complete image of the master being, but also his character. They can also accomplish on their own everything that the master person would want to, while an ordinary being is governed by no one. When people see Law Bodies they find them to be complete, independent, realistic individual lives. Put simply, my Law Bodies are in fact me.

Li Hongzhi
July 21, 1996

Buddha-Nature and Demon-Nature

In a very high and very microscopic dimension of the universe there exist two different kinds of substances. They are two forms of material existence manifest by the supreme nature of the universe, Zhen-Shan-Ren, at certain dimensional levels in the universe. They pervade certain dimensions from top to bottom, or from the microscopic level to the macroscopic level. With regard to the Fa's manifestations at different levels, the lower the level, the greater the difference in the manifestations and variations of these two different substances. As a result, it brings forth what the Dao School calls the principles of *yin* and *yang* and Taiji. Descending further to lower levels, these two kinds of matter with different properties become increasingly opposed to each other, and this then gives rise to the principle of mutual-generation and mutual-inhibition.

Through mutual-generation and mutual-inhibition there appear kindness and wickedness, right and wrong, and good and evil. Then, as to living beings, if there are Buddhas, there are demons; if there are humans, there are ghosts—this is more obvious and complicated in the society of everyday people. Where there are good people, there are bad ones; where there are selfless people, there are selfish ones; where there are open-minded people, there are narrow-minded ones. As to cultivation, where there are people who believe in it, there are people who do not; where there are people who can be enlightened, there are people who cannot; where there are people for it, there are people against it—this is human society. If everyone could practice cultivation, be enlightened to it, and believe in it, human society would turn into a society of gods. Human society is just a society of human beings, and it is not allowed to cease to exist. Human society will continue to exist forever. Therefore, it is normal that there are people who oppose it. It would be abnormal if instead no one objected.

Without ghosts, how could humans reincarnate as humans? Without the existence of demons, one would be unable to cultivate Buddhahood. Without bitterness, there could not be sweetness.

When people try to accomplish something, they encounter difficulty precisely because the principle of mutual-generation and mutual-inhibition exists. Only when you accomplish what you want through bitter effort and overcome difficulties will you find it not easily won, cherish what you have achieved, and feel happy. Otherwise, if there were no principle of mutual-generation and mutual-inhibition and you could accomplish anything without effort, you would feel bored with life and lack a sense of happiness and the joy of success.

Any kind of matter or life in the universe is composed of microscopic particles that make up larger particles, and these then form surface matter. Within the scope covered by these two kinds of matter of differing properties, all matter and lives possess dual nature just the same. For instance, iron and steel are hard, but they oxidize and rust when buried in the earth. Pottery and porcelain, on the other hand, do not oxidize when buried in the earth, but are fragile and easily broken. The same applies to human beings, who possess Buddha-nature and demon-nature at the same time. What one does without moral obligations and constraints is of demon-nature. Cultivating Buddhahood is to eliminate your demon-nature and strengthen and increase your Buddha-nature.

One's Buddha-nature is Shan, and it manifests itself as compassion, thinking of others before acting, and the ability to endure suffering. One's demon-nature is viciousness, and it manifests as killing, stealing and robbing, selfishness, evil thoughts, sowing discord, stirring up troubles by spreading rumors, jealousy, wickedness, anger, laziness, incest and so on.

Being the nature of the universe, Zhen-Shan-Ren manifests in different ways at different levels. The two different kinds of substances within certain levels of the universe also have different manifesting forms at different levels. The lower the level, the more marked the mutual-opposition, and thus the distinction between good and bad. The virtuous becomes more virtuous, while the evil becomes more evil. The dual nature in the same physical subject also becomes more complicated and changeable. This is exactly what Buddha referred to when he said, "Everything has Buddha-nature." In fact, everything has demon-nature as well.

Nevertheless, the universe is characterized by Zhen-Shan-Ren, and so is the society of everyday people. These two kinds of substances that I discussed are nothing but two types of substances that exist from top to bottom, from the microscopic level to the macroscopic level, to human society, and are reflected in living beings and matter and can cause dual nature in them. But lives and matter from the top to the bottom, to human society, are composed of countless varieties of matter from the microscopic level to the macroscopic level.

If mankind does not observe human moral standards, society will enter uncontrollable chaos, with natural calamities and man-made disasters. If a cultivator does not get rid of his demon-nature through cultivation, his *gong* will be badly disordered and he will attain nothing or follow a demonic path.

Li Hongzhi
August 26, 1996

Huge Exposure

A large number of practitioners have now achieved or are about to achieve Consummation. How solemn it is for a human being to achieve Consummation! Nothing in this world could be more wonderful, glorious, or magnificent than this. So it is that strict requirements must be applied to every cultivator in the course of cultivation. Moreover, elevating to each higher level is accomplished by solidly reaching their standards. In terms of the overall situation, Dafa practitioners are qualified, but there are also some people who are fumbling along with various attachments that they have not let go of. Superficially, they too say that Dafa is good, but in reality they do not practice cultivation. This is especially so when the general climate is one where everyone says Dafa is good, as everyone—from the upper classes of society to the common people—speaks highly of it. Some governments also say good things about it that are echoed by the public. Who are the sincere ones, then? Who are merely echoing others' voices? Who sings its praises while actually undermining it? We have changed the situation in human society and reversed the general climate: Now let's see who still says that Dafa is good, and who changes his mind. This way, won't everything suddenly become crystal clear?

From the incident with the *Guangming Daily* until now, every Dafa disciple has played a role: some were determined to steadfastly cultivate; some wrote without reservation to the authorities for the sake of Dafa's reputation; some spoke out against the injustice done by the irresponsible report. But there are also some who have not cultivated their inner selves amidst difficult situations, but have engaged in divisive activities, making the current situation more complicated. Some even stopped cultivating, fearing that their own reputations and self-interest would be harmed. Still others circulated rumors without any concern for Dafa's stability, worsening factors that undermine the Fa. There were also a number of key contact persons in different regions who analyzed Dafa's situation with the unhealthy habit of observing social trends, a habit developed over years of political struggle. By relating isolated problems that arose in different regions, they concluded that some sorts of social trends were unfolding and so they intentionally communicated this to practitioners. Although there were various reasons for this, could anything damage the Fa more seriously? Even worse, some people stirred up trouble by creating rumors with their demon-nature, as though the situation were not chaotic enough.

Dafa belongs to the universe and penetrates all the way down to human society. When a Fa of this magnitude is taught, how could there be anything not be arranged? Isn't what has happened a test for Dafa disciples' *xinxing*? What is cultivation? When you say it's good, I say it's good, and everyone says it's good, how could you see a person's heart? Only at the critical moment can we see his heart. Without letting go of some attachments, he might even dare to betray Buddha—could this be a minor problem? Some people were scared. But what were you afraid of? My disciples! Didn't you hear me say that when a person succeeded in cultivating Arhatship, he stumbled because he developed fear in his heart? Every human attachment must be abandoned, no matter what it is. Some disciples said: "What's there to fear? My body would still sit there even with my head cut off." When you compare them, it is clear with one look how well they cultivate. Of course, some key contact persons are concerned for the safety of Dafa, and this is another story.

We just want to make those disciples who aren't practicing cultivation diligently see their own shortcomings, make those who are stumbling along surface, expose those who undermine the Fa in a disguised way, and enable those who are genuine disciples to reach Consummation.

Li Hongzhi
August 28, 1996

Cultivation Practice is Not Politics

Some practitioners are discontent with society and politics; they learn our Dafa with this strong attachment that they don't abandon. They even attempt to take advantage of our Dafa and get involved in politics—an act born of a filthy mindset—revealing their irreverence toward Buddha and the Fa. They certainly won't reach Consummation if they don't abandon that mindset.

In my lectures I have repeatedly stressed that the form of human society—no matter what type of society or political situation—is predestined and determined by heaven. A cultivator does not need to mind the affairs of the human world, let alone get involved in political struggles. Isn't how society treats us testing cultivators' hearts? We should not get involved in politics.

Such is the form of our Dafa cultivation practice. We will not rely on any political powers at home or abroad. Those people of influence are not cultivators, so they certainly cannot hold any positions of responsibility in our Dafa—either in name or reality.

My disciples, you must remember that we're truly practicing cultivation! We should abandon those ordinary human concerns for reputation, profit, and emotion. Do the conditions of a social system have anything to do with your cultivation practice? You can only reach Consummation after you have abandoned all your attachments and none of them remain. Other than doing a good job with his work, a cultivator will not be interested in politics or political power of any sort; failing this, he absolutely isn't my disciple.

We're able to have cultivators obtain the Fa and achieve the Righteous Attainment, just as we're able to teach people to be kindhearted in society—this is good for the stability of human society. Yet Dafa is not taught for the sake of human society, but for you to reach Consummation.

Li Hongzhi
September 3, 1996

A Person in Charge is Also a Cultivator

The persons in charge of our assistance centers in different regions are those who can work hard for Dafa without complaint. Yet many of these persons just cannot seem to get along well with one another, and so fail to cooperate in their work. This has done great harm to the image of Dafa people have in their minds. Some have asked me "Is because those persons are incapable of doing the work?" I say that's how an ordinary human would put it. The crucial reason is that you, as coordinators and assistant coordinators of the centers, are cultivators who also have attachments that you can't abandon, and you need an environment to get rid of them. But when a tensions arise among those in charge, you usually use the excuse of "not cooperating in the work" or "working for Dafa" to push it aside, instead of seizing this good opportunity to search within and improve yourself. As you didn't let go of your attachments or improve yourselves, the problem will recur again next time. This will surely interfere with your work for Dafa. Don't you know that the tensions among those in charge are arranged by me for you to improve yourselves? Yet you use your work for Dafa to hide the attachment that you should have done better with. You grieve to me in your mind when the problems become too serious to overcome. Do you know how I feel about it at that time? It's not that just because you're the coordinator of a center and work for Dafa you can reach Consummation without having to improve your *xinxing*. Even a practitioner can realize that he's improving his *xinxing* in any disagreement—why can't the coordinator of a center? In order for you to improve, your heart has to be provoked when problems arise; otherwise it won't do. Working for Dafa is also a good opportunity for you to improve your *xinxing*!

Why do I specifically write this article for you? Because every act and every statement of yours directly affects practitioners. If you are doing well in your cultivation, you will do well in spreading the Fa in your local area and practitioners will do better in their cultivation. If this isn't the case, you will harm the Fa. As you are Dafa's elite at the level of everyday people, I can't just let you work without reaching Consummation.

Li Hongzhi
September 3, 1996

What is Cultivation Practice?

When it comes to cultivation practice, many people believe that cultivation practice is only about doing some exercises, sitting in meditation, and learning some incantations that can then transform them into Gods or Buddhas, or allow them to attain the Dao. In fact, that's not cultivation practice but merely practicing for worldly skills.

In religion, much attention is given to cultivation, and this is called "conduct cultivation." Then it goes to the other extreme. A monk or a nun tries hard to chant the scriptures, and he or she regards a person's depth of scripture understanding as the means to reaching Consummation. In fact, when Buddha Sakyamuni, Jesus, and Lao Zi were in this world, there were no scriptures at all—there was only actual cultivation. What the venerable masters taught was to guide cultivation practice. Later followers recalled their words, put them into books, and called them scriptures. They gradually began to study Buddhist philosophy or theories of Dharma. Unlike what went on in the days of those venerable masters—when people would actually practice cultivation and use their teachings as the guide for their cultivation—these people have instead taken the study of religious scriptures and scholarship as cultivation practice.

This is a lesson from history. The disciples who practice cultivation in Falun Dafa must remember that you absolutely should not take the Fa merely as ordinary human academic scholarship or as something for monks to study, rather than actually practicing cultivation. Why do I tell you to study, read, and memorize *Zhuan Falun*? To guide your cultivation! As to those who only do the exercises but don't study the Fa, they are not disciples of Dafa whatsoever. Only when you are studying the Fa and cultivating

62

your heart and mind in addition to the means of reaching Consummation—the exercises, and truly changing yourself fundamentally while improving your *xinxing* and elevating your level—can it be called true cultivation practice.

Li Hongzhi
September 6, 1996

Dafa Will Forever be Pure Like Diamond

Religion cannot be mingled with politics, or its leader will necessarily be preoccupied with worldly affairs. Paying lip service to teaching people's hearts to be good and leading people back to the pure land, these people's hearts are bound to be evil and hypocritical; what they pursue is surely fame and self-interest. Power is what everyday people crave, while fame is a great obstacle to reaching Consummation. This person is bound to gradually become the leader of an evil religion. Because religion's goal is to teach people to be good so that they can eventually return to their heavenly paradise, the principles it preaches must be higher than those in human society. If they are applied to politics in the human world, it is the most serious corruption of heavenly principles. How could Gods and Buddhas be driven by human attachments and involved in the dirty political matters and power struggles of human society? This is what a human being does when driven by his demon-nature. Such a religion is bound to be used by governments to engage in violence and launch religious wars, thereby becoming an evil religion that harms mankind.

Having "all people practice religion" will not do, either. First, this can easily alter religious doctrines and reduce them to theories of ordinary human society. Second, religion can easily be turned into a political

63

tool that will tarnish the Buddha Fa's image. Third, religious leaders will become politicians, and this will make religion come to an end, thereby turning it into an evil religion.

Falun Dafa is not a religion, but future generations will regard it as one. It is taught to human beings for the purpose of cultivation practice, rather than to establish a religion. There can be a large number of people learning Dafa, but it isn't permitted to turn all of a nation's citizens into religious followers and make everyone take part in the unified activities of cultivation practice. Dafa cultivation practice is always voluntary. Never force anyone to participate in cultivation practice.

At no time in the future may Dafa be used for any political matters. Dafa can make people's hearts become good, thus stabilizing society. But by no means is it taught for the purpose of maintaining the things of human society. Disciples, keep in mind that no matter how much pressure there might be in the future from political forces and other powers, Dafa can never be used by political powers.

Never get involved in politics, nor interfere with state affairs. Truly cultivate and become benevolent. Keep Dafa pure, unchanged, and indestructible like diamond, and it will thereby exist forever.

Li Hongzhi
September 7, 1996

Further Understanding

I couldn't have explained the matter of Buddha-nature and demon-nature to you any clearer. The tests you have passed were in fact meant for you to remove your demon-nature. Regardless, from time to time you have used various excuses or Dafa itself to hide it, and failed to improve your *xinxing* while missing opportunities again and again.

Do you realize that as long as you're a cultivator, in any environment or under any circumstances, I will use any troubles or unpleasant things you come across—even if they involve work for Dafa, or no matter how good or sacred you think they are—to eliminate your attachments and expose your demon-nature so that it can be eliminated, for your improvement is what's most important.

If you are able to succeed in improving yourself this way, what you do then, with a pure heart, will be the best and most sacred.

Li Hongzhi
September 9, 1996

Cautionary Advice

It has been four years since I began teaching Dafa. Some practitioners' *xinxing* and level of realm have improved slowly; they remain at the perceptual stage in their understanding of me and Dafa, always being grateful towards me for the changes in their bodies and for the manifestation of supernormal abilities— that is an ordinary human mindset. If you do not want to change your human state and rationally rise to a true understanding of

Dafa, you will miss the opportunity. If you do not change the human logic that you, as an ordinary human, have formed deep in your bones over thousands of years, you will be unable to break away from this superficial human shell and reach Consummation. You cannot always count on me to eliminate karma for you while you fail to truly progress in comprehending the Fa and rise above human understandings and notions. Your ways of thinking, your understanding, and your appreciation toward me and Dafa are the product of ordinary human thinking. But what I am teaching you is in fact moving beyond ordinary humans to a rational, true understanding of Dafa!

In practicing cultivation, you are not making real, solid progress on your own, which would effect great, fundamental changes internally. Instead, you rely on my power and take advantage of powerful external factors. This can never transform your human nature into Buddha-nature. If every one of you can understand the Fa from the depths of your mind, that will truly be the manifestation of the Fa whose power knows no boundary—the reappearance of the mighty Buddha Fa in the human world!

Li Hongzhi
September 10, 1996

Dafa Can Never be Plagiarized

My disciples! I have been repeatedly saying that imparting Dafa to human beings is already the greatest mercy to them. This is something unprecedented in billions of years! Yet some people simply don't realize that they should treasure it. There are others who even want to alter the Fa or the exercises to make them

66

something that belongs to them, their ethnicity, or their nation. Think about it! You think that it's good because of the self-interest that you're attached to or the interests of your nationality and the like—this is an ordinary human mindset. It would be all right if you were dealing with things of ordinary human society, but this isn't something of ordinary humans! The Fa isn't taught for your nationality. This is the universe's Dafa, the fundamental Buddha Fa! It's imparted to human beings to save them. Yet you alter a Fa this great...? To alter just a bit of it is already a colossal sin. Be sure to never generate an evil thought simply because of your attachments to ordinary human society! This is extremely dangerous!

Did you know that in recent years some practitioners suddenly died? Some of them died precisely because they did such things. Don't think that your master might do something to you. You should know that there are numerous guardian gods of the Fa at various levels whose duty is to safeguard the Fa. Furthermore, demons won't leave you alone either! It's because you practice cultivation in the upright Fa that you have escaped the karma you owed in your previous lives. Once you are reduced to the level of an everyday person, no one will protect you and demons will also take your life. It's even useless to seek protection with other Buddhas, Daos, and Gods, as they won't protect someone who undermines the Fa. What's more, your karma will also be returned to your body.

It's difficult to practice cultivation, yet very easy to fall. When a person fails a test or can't let go of a strong human attachment, he might reverse himself and take up the opposite ground. There are too many lessons in history. Only after having fallen down will a person begin to regret, yet then it's too late.

Li Hongzhi
September 22, 1996 in Bangkok

What is Enlightenment?

Enlightenment is also called the Awakening of Wisdom. In our Dafa it is called the Unlocking of Gong; that is, one has reached Consummation through cultivation, finished the entire course of cultivation, and is about to go to a heavenly paradise.

What state is an enlightened being in after Enlightenment? One who has succeeded in cultivating Buddhahood will become a Buddha; one who has succeeded in cultivating Bodhisattvahood will become a Bodhisattva; one who has succeeded in cultivating Arhatship will become an Arhat; one who cultivates the Dao will attain the Dao; and one who has succeeded in cultivating Godhood will already be a God. Because after reaching Consummation some enlightened beings still have something to do in the society of everyday people or some wishes to fulfill, they need to live among everyday people for a period of time. But living like that among everyday people is hard for them. Because they are far too different from everyday people in their realm of thought, they are able to detect clearly all the evil thoughts in the minds of everyday people, including their strong attachments, selfishness, dirtiness, and scheming against others. Also, they can simultaneously detect the slightest mind activities of thousands of people. Furthermore, karma and viruses are everywhere in the society of everyday people; there are also many other bad things floating in the air, unknown to human beings. They can see all these clearly. The karma in the present human society of Last Havoc is quite enormous. While breathing, people inhale large amounts of karma, viruses, and poisonous gases. It is indeed very difficult for them to stay in this ordinary human world.

So what are they like? This is what those practitioners who are attached to this matter try to figure out. Don't try to figure out whether this person looks like an enlightened being or that person looks like someone who has reached Consummation. You should put your mind to diligently and truly cultivating and reach Consummation sooner. Why look at others? As a matter of fact, those enlightened people are often disciples who don't show themselves off but who quietly and truly cultivate. They are of different ages and look no different from everyday people. It is very likely that they don't attract much attention. Although they possess all the divine powers and abilities of transformation, they find that human beings actually look like tiny, low beings who don't deserve to be shown these things. Moreover, human beings would develop various petty human understandings and thoughts if they were to see these things, treating them with the human attachment of zealotry; enlightened beings cannot stand this. It is difficult for everyday people to understand wherein lies the true significance of the inner meaning of Buddha Fa's divine powers.

At present, some practitioners who care about too many things other than being diligent in cultivation are searching everywhere for enlightened persons and so on. Think about it, everyone: The enlightened ones are already Buddhas and possess everything a Buddha should have. How could they casually allow people to know about them? How could humans know about Buddhas? When you are searching everywhere for them, your attachments, competitiveness, curiosity, desire to show off and your being meddlesome, combined with the desire to pursue, are at the same time interfering with practitioners' peaceful cultivation. So do you know how they feel about this? Every intentional human act or thought makes them feel uncomfortable!

Because some practitioners have come from very high dimensions to obtain the Fa, they will become Enlightened very soon. The two-year time for cultivation practice that I mentioned was for these disciples. But all our Dafa disciples have indeed made rapid progress in true cultivation. Many of them will soon become enlightened, which is beyond the imagination of cultivators before. I hope everyone will maintain a peaceful mind and make continual progress with perseverance. As each person reaches Consummation, I will receive and deliver each.

Li Hongzhi
September 26, 1996

Remaking Mankind

The reality known by man is an illusion created by his ignorant view of history's development and by the empirical sciences. It is not the true manifestation of the great reality within the universe. Furthermore, the genuine reality is bound to bring about a new science and a new understanding. The laws and principles of the universe will appear again in the human world.

Human selfishness, greed, stupidity, and ignorance are interwoven with the goodness inherent in human nature, and humans are unknowingly creating everything they will have to bear; this is currently swallowing up society. Numerous social problems of various sorts are surfacing in the world and crises lurk everywhere. Yet man does not know to find the causes within his own nature. After the degeneration of morality, man is unable to see that the terrible human heart is the poisonous root of social problems, and so man always foolishly tries to find the way out in social phenomena. As a result, man never realizes that all the so-called "ways out" that he creates for himself are precisely him sealing himself off. As such, there are even fewer ways out, and the new problems that follow are even worse. Thus, with much difficulty man again finds a tiny space and takes new measures, thereby closing this remaining bit of space once again. As this repeats itself over a period of time, there is no room left and he can no longer find a way out, nor can he see the truth beyond the enclosed space. Man begins to suffer from all that he has created for himself. This is the final way in which the universe eliminates lives.

The Lord of Buddhas, whose mercy is incredibly immense, has left the Buddha Fa to man. The universe is giving man another opportunity, allowing the mighty Buddha Fa once again to reveal the universe's actual reality to the human world, to wash away all filth and ignorance, and to use human language to recapture its brilliance and splendor. May you cherish it! The Buddha Fa is right in front of you.

Li Hongzhi
September 28, 1996

Degeneration

The clergy's misconduct completely violates the vows of purity they have taken, makes God's entrustment not worth even a penny, and astonishes both mankind and gods. Kindhearted people have been regarding them as the only people whom they can rely on for salvation. Disappointment has made people increasingly disbelieve in religion, and in the end people have completely lost their faith in God, thereby committing all kinds of bad deeds without any reservations. This has evolved to the extent that people today have completely turned into depraved people who manifest demonic furor, and this has made all gods completely lose their confidence in man. This is one of the main reasons why gods no longer look after human beings.

Li Hongzhi
October 10, 1996

Non-Omission in Buddha-Nature

In teaching the Fa, I have mentioned many times that the appearance of scriptures in Sakyamuni's Buddhism and in the Dharma-Ending Period was brought about mainly because some people added into the Dharma their own words and understandings—this is the greatest lesson in history. Nevertheless, some disciples simply refuse to abandon their ordinary human attachments. Being taken advantage of by the demon-nature of being attached to showing off their eloquence and literary talents, they unknowingly undermine the Buddha Fa.

Recently, some people have been calling it "dumping dirty water" when practitioners, after deepening their understanding in their cultivation, speak of their past shortcomings in sharing their experiences. This has completely changed the content of cultivation practice. Cultivation practice is sacred, and it is not something like an everyday person's self-examination or repentance. Disciples! You should not casually take up a term used or mentioned by everyone. Isn't this adding something human to Dafa? Last year, after the Beijing assistance center put forward the four phrases, I wrote an article, "Correction," specifically for it. It should be taken seriously. Of course, there are still some other improper terms being circulated. You should think about it: If one word is added today and another the day after tomorrow, with the passage of time the next generation of disciples will not be able to tell whose words they are, and gradually Dafa will be changed.

You must be clear that the form of cultivation practice that I leave you can never be altered. Don't do anything that I do not, and don't use anything that I do not. In cultivation you should say things however I say them. Pay attention! Inadvertent alteration of the Buddha Fa is undermining it all the same!

I also want to tell you that your nature in the past was actually based on egotism and selfishness. From now on, whatever you do, you should consider others first, so as to attain the righteous Enlightenment of selflessness and altruism. So from now on, whatever you do or whatever you say, you must consider others—or even future generations—along with Dafa's eternal stability.

Li Hongzhi
February 13, 1997

Clearheaded

It is time to make a few remarks on the current methods of work employed by assistance center coordinators in different regions. It is correct to implement the requirements of the Research Society, but you should mind the way you do it. I often say that if all a person wants is the well-being of others and if this is without the slightest personal motivation or personal understanding, what he says will move the listener to tears. I have not only taught you Dafa, but have also left you my demeanor. While working, your tone of voice, your kindheartedness, and your reasoning can change a person's heart, whereas commands never could! If others are not convinced deep down inside but only superficially comply, they will still conduct themselves according to their own will when no one is around to see them.

Any work in Dafa is intended for people to obtain the Fa and for disciples to improve themselves. Anything other than these two points is meaningless. Therefore, all activities should be organized according to local conditions and practitioners' situations, instead of being made absolute. Even learning Dafa is voluntary, not to mention organizing activities! As a matter of fact, the person in charge of a center is first of all a leader in studying the Fa. If a person does not study the Fa well himself, he will not do a good job in his work. The experience sharing conferences organized by assistance centers in different regions should never be turned into self-criticism conferences. Such solemn Fa Conferences for sharing cultivation experiences in Dafa should never be turned into exhibitional conferences for exposing the dark side of society, still less should you force practitioners to reveal the shortcomings they had and mistakes they made when they were everyday people; you would thereby inflict serious, negative effects, damaging Dafa's reputation. You should be clear on what you should do and what you should not do. This is solemn cultivation practice. The experience sharing conferences are intended for the improvement of practitioners and the promotion of Dafa, but not for publicizing how bad our practitioners once were. They are for talking about practicing Dafa cultivation, not dumping so-called "dirty water!" The work you do for Dafa is not irrelevant to your cultivation practice. Factors that are to improve your *xinxing* appear everywhere in your work. You should not only do your work, but also reach Consummation. I know that a few of you seldom read the books or study the Fa, nor do you examine yourselves according to the several articles I have written for you that you call scriptures. What are the "scriptures"? They are simply articles to be read frequently. Do you read them? If you study the Fa more, you will not do a bad job in your work. I point out your shortcomings in order to make Dafa develop in a more healthy way, with fewer problems. In fact, Dafa is also enriching you and creating the elite of Dafa.

Li Hongzhi
June 13, 1997 in Hong Kong.

Bear in Mind Forever

Dafa Society:

I suggest that every disciple immediately, on the spot, destroy everything that I have not publicly issued but that is in circulation without permission, such as: my speeches that came out of Chengde; what a practitioner from Beijing said about supernormal abilities; the speech of the assistance center coordinator in Dalian; the cave story from the coordinator of the Guizhou assistance center and other speeches; not to mention the speeches made by people in charge of different regions; what was said by practitioners after seeing me; the speech given by people in charge of the Dafa Research Society, and so on, plus texts, recordings, videotapes, etc., that have been transcribed from my speeches without permission. All these must be destroyed on the spot, and they cannot be kept regardless of the excuse. What is "safeguarding Dafa"? This is most thoroughly a safeguarding of Dafa, and a test of whether you can follow what I tell you and whether you are truly my disciples! Let me tell everyone once again that the Dharma taught by Buddha Sakyamuni was sabotaged this way. This is a lesson in history. From now on, nobody should tape-record or videotape speeches given by any of the people in charge in different regions or by any disciples; even less can they be edited into texts or be spread around for people to read. This is not a problem of any particular person, nor is this to criticize any person in particular here; instead, this is rectifying Dafa. Bear in mind: except for Dafa practitioners' experience sharing conferences for studying the Fa and activities organized by major assistance centers with the endorsement of the Research Society, anything that does not belong to Dafa but is being circulated in Dafa undermines Dafa.

Li Hongzhi
June 18, 1997

A Heavy Blow

To make it convenient for more people to practice cultivation, Dafa at present mainly takes the form of cultivation practice in the society of everyday people; practitioners temper themselves in their workplaces and other environments of everyday person. Only monks and nuns need to roam around. Yet some people are now traveling all over the country and calling themselves Dafa disciples. They live in the homes of Dafa disciples for no reason, while eating, drinking, taking, and asking for things. Swindling and bluffing, they take advantage of Dafa by capitalizing on the kind nature of practitioners. But why can't our practitioners distinguish them? Practicing cultivation is to cultivate one's own self. Think about it: Why don't these people do actual cultivation calmly in their own homes? A difficult environment can help a person cultivate himself better. Why do these people disregard my words and move around the whole country? Why do these people eat, take, and ask for practitioners' things, yet ask them to abandon their attachments? Is this what I've taught them? Even worse, some stay in practitioners' homes for a few consecutive months. Isn't this flagrantly interfering with and harming practitioners' cultivation practice? I think that these people need to pay back in full what they have eaten and taken by swindling. Dafa won't permit it to be otherwise. If this sort of thing occurs again in the future, you can treat that person as a regular swindler and report him to the police, for that person absolutely is not our practitioner.

Also, in some regions people have organized so-called "Fa-preaching groups" without permission, acting pretentiously among practitioners and swindling people everywhere. There are people who also invite individuals to give speeches, thereby undermining and interfering with practitioners' cultivation. On the surface these people appear to be spreading Dafa, but in reality they are promoting themselves. A practitioner's cultivation is arranged systematically by my Law Bodies. It is only that some practitioners don't know this or they remain unaware of it. So aren't these people causing interference? It is especially difficult for those who have just started learning the Fa to make a clear distinction. There are also people delivering so-called "speeches" in conferences that are attended by thousands. What they have said was all about themselves. They even define some sentences of Dafa or interpret Dafa, with their bodies emitting to the practitioners black karma and attachment substances. I have stated explicitly in *Zhuan Falun* that this is forbidden. Why don't you think about this? This is especially so for those who are in charge of hosting and have invited people to do those things, for you might have inflicted some intangible harm to Dafa disciples, and you are no longer qualified to be in charge of Dafa disciples. Without listening to me or following the requirements of Dafa, how could you be my disciples? Isn't this going against Dafa? If this isn't an act of harming to Dafa, what is it? My disciples, you shouldn't always be unaware of these things until I point them out. In fact, everything is included in the Fa. Why not read the books more? I suggest that everyone set his mind to reading ten times the book I wrote, *Essentials for Further Advancement*, which you call scripture. When your mind isn't at peace, studying the Fa is not effective. You should study it with a peaceful mind.

In a few regions we have people in charge who don't read the books or study the Fa. What's more, they claim that they have headaches whenever they read the Fa. Isn't it obvious that demons are interfering with them, and yet they don't want to break from their control? Even a new practitioner can realize this. How can such people be in charge? I think it is better for people like that to voluntarily become common practitioners and actually practice cultivation for a period of time peacefully—this is good for both Dafa and them. There was also someone who understood my letter of criticism to her in the opposite way. She made copies and distributed them to show off, without realizing her mistake. She claimed, "Teacher even wrote to me." Also, in order to have practitioners follow their commands, some people often use words in their speeches like, "On behalf of Teacher Li, I ...," and so on. Nobody can represent me. How could your words become my words? What I say is the Fa. Could what you say become the Fa? My disciples! I suggest that you first become common practitioners for a period of time, and then resume your work after becoming clearheaded. No matter how much work a person in charge has done among everyday people, he is working for Dafa out of his own will. The success of his work is only a manifestation among ordinary humans. It is the mighty power of Dafa itself and the specific arrangements made by my Law Bodies that enable people to obtain the Fa and spread the Fa widely. Without my Law Bodies doing these things, even protecting the people in charge can hardly be ensured, let alone spreading the Fa widely. So don't always think of yourselves too highly. There is no fame, self-interest, or official titles in Dafa, but only cultivation practice.

Li Hongzhi
June 18, 1997

Another Comment on Evaluation Criteria

Recently, there have been a great number of new practitioners who have not yet gained a deeper understanding of Dafa's requirements. There are some regions in particular where the Dafa practitioners in charge are new, too. Therefore, within a very short time you are required to study the Fa in depth so that all your conduct and your demeanor will conform to Dafa. Meanwhile, the general assistance centers in different regions need to be careful selecting people. Those who mislead practitioners should be replaced as soon as possible, and those who study Dafa well should be selected to take charge.

Of late, some assistance centers have asked those whose Third Eye *(tianmu)* are said to be open to examine practitioners' cultivation. Everything those people have seen is in fact false and illusory. I said long ago that the criterion for evaluating a practitioner was nothing but his *xinxing*, and I will never allow anyone who hasn't attained Enlightenment or reached Consummation to see clearly my disciples' actual cultivation states. What is visible to those who can see are merely manifestations shown to them at their particular low levels, and they are unable to see things at higher levels. If someone in charge uses such a person to examine other practitioners, this person will develop an attachment to showing off. Moreover, his demon-nature will also cause interference and damage, so what he sees will be transformed by his mind activities. It was wrong for him to examine Dafa disciples in the first place. The person in charge who asked him to examine practitioners also didn't follow my words. Why don't you listen to your Master's words: "The only criterion for evaluating a practitioner's cultivation is his *xinxing*"? Don't you know that all dimensions exist simultaneously in the same place? Living beings in any dimension are likely to overlap with human bodies, and they look very much like possessing spirits (*futi*). Yet they exist in different dimensions and have nothing to do with humans. Can those whose Third Eye are said to be open understand these complex situations?

Also, some people casually claim that this person has spirit possession or that person has spirit possession. Let me tell you that the problem lies in those who make such statements themselves.

This universe's dimensions are extremely complex. What I have said has exhausted all expressions of human language. A lot of situations are beyond the description of human language. Even a disciple who has reached Consummation can only see clearly what he has enlightened to at his Attainment Status, not to mention a person who is still practicing cultivation.

Li Hongzhi
June 18, 1997

Definitive Conclusion

Dafa disciples, you must bear in mind that in the future any behavior such as dividing Dafa into branches, schools, sects, or denominations, by anyone, at any time, in any place, and with any excuse, is undermining the Fa. You should never do what I don't allow you to. The desire to show off plus the attachment of zealotry are most easily exploited by the demonic part of your mind. Whatever you have enlightened to in Dafa is no more than a tiny portion of the Fa's principles at a certain level within the boundless Fa's principles. You must never define the Fa or a part of it—not even a sentence of it. If you do that in public, the moment you utter it you will have produced sinful karma. In serious cases, the sin can be as big as a mountain or the sky—how could you then cultivate yourself? If one alters Dafa and creates another system, his sin will be so great that it is boundless. When a life is paying for that evil karma, the pain from its being eliminated layer after layer will be eternal and endless.

Dafa can rectify the universe, so it certainly has the Fa's power to repress evil, eliminate disorder, harmonize everything, and remain invincible. As a matter of fact, there have been many lessons in this regard. Things that undermine the Fa will be handled by gods who safeguard the Fa. When all sentient beings treasure Dafa, they are treasuring their own lives and being compassionate to all sentient beings. Dafa is unchangeable and unshakable. It will live forever and always exist in the world. Heaven and earth will remain stable forever.

Li Hongzhi
July 1, 1997

A Dialogue with Time

Master: What problems do you find my disciples to still have?

Divine Being: Your disciples can be divided into two groups.

Master: What are the two groups?

Divine Being: One group is able to painstakingly make progress in the Fa by following your requirements. This group is quite good. The other group is attached to human matters, is unwilling to give them up, and is unable to steadfastly make progress.

Master: Yes, I've seen that.

Divine Being: You allow them a period of time to understand the Fa, so some people come with various intentions. After studying the Fa, most of them are able to change their initial purpose for learning the Fa.

Master: Some of them have not changed yet.

Divine Being: Yet it has been too long a time.

Master: Yes!

Divine Being: In my opinion, there is no need to wait for those who cannot become gods. In fact, they can only be humans.

Master: (talking to himself) In the human world, they are indeed too thoroughly lost. They might have to end up like this. I'm afraid they won't even be qualified to be humans in the end!

Divine Being: Actually it's not bad to become humans in the new world. Compared with those innumerable high-level beings in the universe who have been eliminated by history, they are already incomparably fortunate.

Master: I still want to wait for some time, see what they are like when the more microscopic matter that damages mankind has been cleaned up, and then make a decision. After all, they did come to obtain the Fa.

Divine Being: In terms of this group of people at present, some have come to study the Fa because they could not find their purpose in life. They are attached to these notions which they are unwilling to change.

Master: There are more such people among new practitioners.

Divine Being: Some of them have come looking for the aspect of the Fa that they consider good, but they are unable to let go of the aspect that prevents them from having a complete understanding of the Fa.

Master: There are also such people among veteran disciples. And the most outstanding evidence of that is that they always compare themselves with humans and with their own past, but fail to examine themselves with the requirements of the Fa at different levels.

Divine Being: These problems have already become very serious. It would be good if they could manage to search within themselves for the things that they have been able to find in others.

Master: It's time for them to become clearheaded so that their environment can turn into one for true cultivation practice, and thus they will be able to become real gods.

Li Hongzhi
July 3, 1997

Expounding on the Fa

For a long period of time the sentient beings in Dafa, especially the disciples, have had a misunderstanding of the Fa at various levels regarding *xinxing* improvement. Whenever a tribulation comes, you do not see it with the side of your original nature but view it completely with your human side. Evil demons then capitalize on this point and inflict endless interference and damage, leaving practitioners in long-term tribulations. As a matter of fact, this results from an inadequate understanding of the Fa by your human side. You have humanly restrained your divine side; in other words, you have restrained the parts that have been successfully cultivated and have prevented them from rectifying the Fa. How can the uncultivated side restrain your main thoughts or the side that has already attained the Fa? Having humanly fostered the evil demons, you allow them to capitalize on the loopholes in the Fa. When a tribulation arrives, if you, a disciple, can truly maintain an unshakable calm or be determined to meet different requirements at different levels, this should be sufficient for you to pass the test. If it continues endlessly and if there do not exist other problems in your *xinxing* or conduct, it must be that the evil demons are capitalizing on the weak spots caused by your lack of control. After all, a cultivator is not an ordinary human. So why doesn't the side of you that is your original nature rectify the Fa?

There are two reasons why Master did not teach this Fa until today: one is that your problem in this regard has become prominent; the other is that you have gained a very deep understanding of the Fa and will not understand it in a simple way.

You should also be clear that "natural" does not exist, and there is a reason for "the inevitable." In fact, "natural" is irresponsibly used by everyday people to make excuses for themselves when they are unable to explain the phenomena of the universe, life, and matter. They cannot imagine what "nature" itself is. Under the influence of this kind of notion you think that all these tribulations are inevitable and that this is just the way it is, thereby developing a passive and pessimistic attitude. So your human side must stay aware. More importantly, your side that has attained the Fa must be clear.

Be aware: I am not asking you to intentionally do something. I am only trying to make you understand the principles of the Fa so that you will have a clear understanding of this. In fact, Dafa is not only to save human beings—it is also taught to all beings in the various dimensions. Your enlightened, original nature will automatically know what to do.

Cherishing your human side enables you to enlighten to and ascend in the Fa. Dafa is harmonizing all sentient beings, and all sentient beings are also harmonizing Dafa. I have told you the solemnity and sacredness of the Fa in order to eliminate your confusion and misunderstanding of the Fa.

Li Hongzhi
July 5, 1997

Abandon Human Attachments and Continue True Cultivation

With the spreading of Dafa, more and more people are able to understand Dafa. So we must pay attention to one matter: Do not bring the human concepts of caste or hierarchy into Dafa. Both veteran and new practitioners must be mindful of this matter. Anyone who comes to study the Fa—no matter how learned he is, how big his business, how high his rank, what special skills he has, or what supernormal abilities he possesses—must actually practice cultivation. Cultivation practice is magnificent and solemn. Whether you can abandon your particular human notions is a major test that you will have difficulty passing, yet you must pass. After all, as a disciple truly practicing cultivation, you must abandon these attachments since you can never reach Consummation without abandoning these notions.

Veteran practitioners should also pay attention to this matter. As more people study the Fa, you should pay more attention to guiding new practitioners to actually practice cultivation. Meanwhile, you yourselves should not slack. If circumstances permit, you can increase the time spent studying the Fa and doing the exercises. Maintaining Dafa's tradition, upholding Dafa's cultivation principles, and persevering in true cultivation are long-term tests for every Dafa disciple.

Li Hongzhi
July 31, 1997

Take the Middle Way

In order to have Dafa disciples avoid deviation in their cultivation practice, whenever a common or serious problem appears, I will write an article to point it out in a timely manner so that disciples may realize it and Dafa will suffer fewer losses. This is because whether we can take the right way does not depend only on disciples' cultivating righteously; whether Dafa's overall form is righteous is also a key factor. So, as your teacher, I will often correct the deviations that occur.

Because of disciples' differences in understanding, some disciples always go from one extreme to the other. Whenever they read the Fa I have written they take extreme actions, thereby causing new problems. When I tell you to change your human understandings, I am not asking you to maintain a human way of understanding Dafa. Yet neither should you be irrational or eccentric. I want you to be clearheaded in understanding Dafa.

Li Hongzhi
August 3, 1997

The Fa Rectifies the Human Heart

As the number of disciples practicing cultivation in Dafa increases, more and more people want to learn about Dafa. Yet some of them do not come here to practice cultivation. Instead, they want to find solutions in Dafa, as they have discovered that there is no way out for human society; this leads to the composition of practitioners as a whole being impure. At the same time, this has also interfered with Dafa from another angle. For instance, some people get some inspiration from Dafa and launch in society something like a civil movement. This kind of Fa-plagiarizing behavior, which originates from Dafa but fails to validate Dafa, works against Dafa from another perspective. As a matter of fact, no movement can bring about a fundamental change in the human heart. Nor do movements' phenomena last—people become indifferent with the passage of time. Afterwards, unhealthy phenomena that are harder to tackle will emerge. Dafa absolutely cannot fall into this kind of condition.

At present, of all the good citizens and good deeds publicized by the media—such as radio, TV, newspapers, etc.—many have been done by our Dafa practitioners since they practice cultivation in Dafa and have improved their *xinxing*. The news reports, however, claim that these people have done so because they are role models or key figures, etc., thereby completely disregarding the fact that their conduct was a result of their practicing Dafa cultivation. This is mainly caused by disciples themselves. Cultivation practice is a great and magnificent thing. Why can't you tell the interviewers in an open and dignified manner that you do those things because you practice Dafa cultivation? If the reporter does not want to mention Dafa, we should not cover up for any form that plagiarizes Dafa and fails to validate it. All of us are trying to be good people, and this is in the interest of society and mankind. Why can't we have a just and legitimate environment? Disciples, you should bear in mind that Dafa is harmonizing you and you are also harmonizing Dafa.

Li Hongzhi
August 17, 1997

Principles for Disciples Who Are Monks and Nuns

Recently, a number of disciples who are monks and nuns in a religion have begun practicing Dafa cultivation. To enable themselves to improve as quickly as possible, they should abandon the bad inclinations modern religions have developed over a long period of time. In this regard, our Dafa disciples practicing cultivation among everyday people should not encourage these people to develop such things. The cultivation method that Buddha Sakyamuni left for monks and nuns was very good. But modern monks and nuns have altered it because many of them could not let go of their attachment to money. They have even made up some excuses to justify themselves over this, such as renovating temples, building Buddha statues, printing Buddhist scriptures, covering the expenses for maintaining temples, and so on. None of these are cultivation practice; instead, they are all intention-filled actions that have nothing to do with actual cultivation. A person absolutely cannot achieve Consummation by means of them.

If you want to cultivate Dafa, you must let go of attachments to money and possessions. Otherwise, how could you meet the standard for being a Dafa disciple? Additionally, except in special situations, disciples who are monks or nuns are not allowed to travel by motor vehicle, plane, or ship. All should travel on foot. Only through enduring hardships can one repay one's karma. You can collect alms with an alms bowl when you are hungry (you should only beg for food, but never for money or goods). At night, you may stay at the homes of Dafa disciples in different regions, but not for long. You must set strict requirements for yourselves! Otherwise, you are not my disciples. Because disciples who are monks or nuns have different cultivation circumstances from those of disciples who practice cultivation at home, society does not treat you as everyday people, either. To achieve Consummation soon, disciples who are monks and nuns should temper themselves in the human world. You should never be attached to comfort or pleasure, nor should you use any excuse to seek fame or gain. Still less should you ask for money to send home. If you cannot abandon worldly thoughts, you should not have become a monk or nun. In ancient times there were very strict requirements for becoming a monk or nun. Dafa disciples who are monks or nuns should set even stricter requirements for themselves. Since you have become a monk or nun, why can't you let go of worldly thoughts?

Disciples! As for disciples practicing cultivation at home, they will gradually, thoroughly abandon attachments to the secular world. But for disciples who are monks or nuns, this is a prerequisite that they must meet from the very beginning, as well as a requirement for becoming a monk or nun.

Li Hongzhi
October 16, 1997

Environment

The cultivation practice form that I have left for Dafa disciples ensures that disciples can truly improve themselves. For example, I ask you to do the exercises as a group in parks in order to form an environment. This environment is the best way to change the surface of a person. The lofty conduct that Dafa disciples have established in this environment—including every word and every deed—can make people recognize their own weaknesses and identify their shortcomings; it can move their hearts, refine their conduct, and enable them to make progress more rapidly. Therefore, new practitioners or self-taught disciples have to go to the practice sites to do the exercises. There are currently about 40 million practitioners in China participating daily in group exercises at the practice sites, and there are tens of millions of veteran disciples who do not go to the practice sites very often (for veteran disciples, this is normal, as this results from their state in cultivation practice). Nevertheless, as new disciples, you should never miss out on this environment. This is because all those whom you come into contact with in society are everyday people. What is more, they are everyday people who have undergone a rapid decline in human morality. In this big dye vat, people can only drift along with the current.

There are also many new Dafa practitioners who are secretly practicing at home, fearing the embarrassment of others finding out. Think about it: What kind of thought is this? An ordinary fear is an attachment that needs to be eliminated through cultivation practice. Yet you are afraid of others finding out that you are learning Dafa? Cultivation practice is a very serious matter. How should you regard yourself and the Fa? There are also some people in leadership positions that find it embarrassing to go out and do the exercises. If you can't even overcome such a trivial feeling, what

91

would you be able to cultivate? In fact, even if you go to the practice site, there might not be people who know you. In some workplaces, almost all the executives are learning Dafa, but no one knows that the others are also learning. The environment is created by you, yourselves, and it, too, is essential for your improvement. I often find that you are in a good state of mind when you study the Fa or do the exercises, but when you come into contact with your work or other people, you become the same as everyday people. You sometimes seem even worse than everyday people. How could this be the conduct of a Dafa disciple?

I want to treat you as my disciples, but what should I do if you, yourselves don't want to be my disciples? Every attachment for you to remove in your cultivation practice is a wall, standing there and blocking your path of cultivation practice. If you cannot be determined about the Fa itself, you cannot practice cultivation. Do not take your position among everyday people too seriously. Do not think that others will fail to understand you if you learn Dafa. Think about it: Even people's claim that they have evolved from apes is able to be highly regarded. Yet with this great Dafa of the universe, you are embarrassed to give it a correct position—this is human beings' true shame.

Li Hongzhi
October 17, 1997

92

Digging Out the Roots

Recently, a few scoundrels from literary, scientific, and *qigong* circles, who have been hoping to become famous through opposing *qigong*, have been constantly causing trouble, as though the last thing they want to see is a peaceful world. Some newspapers, radio stations and TV stations in various parts of the country have directly resorted to these propaganda tools to harm our Dafa, having a very bad impact on the public. This was deliberately harming Dafa and cannot be ignored. Under these very special circumstances, Dafa disciples in Beijing adopted a special approach to ask those people to stop harming Dafa—this actually was not wrong. This is only to be done in extremely restricted situations (other regions should not copy their approach). But when practitioners voluntarily approach those uninformed and irresponsible media agencies and explain to them our true situation, this should not be considered wrong.

What I would like to tell you is not whether this incident itself was right or wrong. Instead, I want to point out that this event has exposed some people. They still have not fundamentally changed their human notions, and they still perceive problems with the human mentality wherein human beings protect human beings. I have said that Dafa absolutely should not get involved in politics. The purpose of this event itself was to help the media understand our actual situation and learn about us positively so that they would not drag us into politics. Speaking from another perspective, Dafa can teach the human heart to be good and it can stabilize society. But you must be clear that Dafa certainly is not taught for these purposes, but rather for cultivation practice.

Dafa has created a way of existence for the lowest level, mankind. Then, among various types of human behavior within the human form of existence at this level, which include collectively presenting facts to someone, and so forth, aren't these one of the numerous forms of existence that Dafa gives to mankind at the lowest level? It is just that when humans do things, good and evil coexist. Thus, there are struggles and politics. Under extremely special circumstances, however, Dafa disciples adopted that approach from the Fa at the lowest level, and they completely applied their good side. Wasn't this an act that harmonized the Fa at the level of mankind? Except under special extreme circumstances, this type of approach is not to be adopted.

I have long noticed that a few individuals do not have the heart to safeguard Dafa, but instead intend to safeguard certain things in human society. If you were an everyday person I would have no objections—it is certainly a good thing to be a good person who safeguards human society. But now you are a cultivator. What standpoint you view Dafa from is fundamental—this is also what I want to point out to you. During your cultivation practice, I will use every means to expose all of your attachments and dig them out at their roots.

You cannot always rely on me to bring you up to a higher level while you, yourself do not move. Only after the Fa is explicitly stated do you make a move. If it is not taught clearly, you do not move, or move backward. I cannot recognize such behavior as cultivation practice. At the crucial moment when I ask you to break away from humanness, you do not follow me. Each opportunity will not occur again. Cultivation practice is a serious matter. The distance has become greater and greater. It is extremely dangerous to add anything human to cultivation practice. In fact, it is also fine to just be a good person. But you must be clear that you choose your own path.

Through this event, it has been observed that several individuals ran around among disciples, doing harm. Instead of thinking correctly and presenting their views kindly to the assistance centers, they spread rumors among practitioners, sowed discord, organized factions, and adopted the worst ordinary human methods. What is more, some people even irrationally tried to drive practitioners away. Some of the practitioners whom you tried to drive away have cultivated themselves many times better than you have. Have you thought about this? Why did you act irrationally with so much anger? Couldn't that mentality enable you to recognize that strong attachment of yours? Let me tell everyone: This Fa is inconceivably enormous, and you will never completely know or understand its laws and principles.

I don't emphasize any specific approach; I use various means to expose your deeply-concealed attachments and get rid of them.

Li Hongzhi
July 6, 1998

For Whom do You Exist?

The most difficult things for people to abandon are their notions. Some people cannot change, even if they have to give up their lives for fake principles. Yet notions are themselves acquired postnatally. People always believe that these unshakable ideas— ideas which can make them pay any price without a second thought— are their own thoughts. Even when they see the truth they reject it. In fact, other than a person's innate purity and innocence, all notions are acquired postnatally and are not a person's actual self.

If these acquired notions become too strong, their role will reverse by dictating a person's true thinking and behavior. At this point, that person might still think that they are his own ideas. This is the case for almost all contemporary people.

In dealing with relevant, important matters, if a life can really assess things without any preconceived notions, then this person is truly able to take charge of himself. This clearheadedness is wisdom, and it is different from what average people call "intelligence." If a person cannot do that, then he is dictated by acquired notions or external thoughts. He might even devote his entire life to struggling for them; but when he gets old, he will not even know what he has been doing in this lifetime. Though he has achieved nothing in his lifetime, he has committed innumerable mistakes while being driven by these acquired notions. Therefore, in his next life he will have to pay for the karma according to his own wrong deeds.

When a person becomes agitated, what controls his thoughts and feelings is not reason, but emotion. When a person's various notions, such as his faith in science, religion, or an ideology, etc., are being challenged by the truth of the Buddha Fa, he will also become agitated. This causes the evil side of human nature to predominate, thereby making him become even more irrational; this is a result of being controlled by the acquired notions. He will blindly jump to conclusions or complicate the matter. Even a person with a predestined relationship can lose the preordained opportunity because of this, turning his own actions into eternal, deep regrets.

Li Hongzhi
July 11, 1998

Melt Into the Fa

At present, more and more people are becoming Dafa practitioners, and there is a trend wherein newcomers have a better perceptual understanding. With no obstacles from the ultra-leftist thinking that existed earlier in society, and without needing process to accept it conceptually, they do not need to spend a great amount of time on discussion during group study of the Fa. So they should spend a great amount of time studying the Fa to elevate themselves as quickly as possible. The more your mind holds, the faster the change.

I once talked about what a good person is and what a bad person is. It is not that one who appears to have committed a bad deed is a bad person and one who has done something good is a good person. Some people's minds are full of bad thoughts—it is just that they have not shown them or have slyly concealed them relatively well; yet these are truly bad people. Some people, on the other hand, are not bad to begin with but occasionally commit wrong deeds; these people are not necessarily bad people. Then how should we understand good people and bad people?

A person is like a container: He is whatever he contains. All of what a person sees with the eyes and hears with the ears are: violence, lust, power struggles in literary works, struggles for profit in the practical world, money worship, other manifestations of demon-nature, and so on. With his head filled with these, this kind of person is truly a bad person, no matter what he appears to be. A person's behavior is dictated by his thoughts. With a mind full of such things, what's a person able to do? It is only because everyone's mind is more or less contaminated to some extent that people cannot detect the problem that has surfaced. Incorrect social trends that are reflected in every aspect of society are imperceptibly changing people, poisoning mankind, and creating a large number of what people call "anti-tradition," "anti-upright," and "anti-moral" human beings with demon-nature. This is what's truly worrisome! Even though society's economy has made progress, it will be ruined in these people's hands since they do not have human ways of thinking.

On the other hand, if a person accepts the kind, traditional thoughts of mankind that have prevailed for thousands of years, believes in proper human behavior and standards, and is filled with all good things, what will this person's conduct be like? Whether or not this person shows it, he is genuinely a good person.

As a practitioner, if his mind is filled with nothing but Dafa, this person is definitely a genuine cultivator. So you must have a clear understanding on the matter of studying the Fa. Reading the books more and studying the books more is the key to truly elevating yourself. To put it more simply, as long as you read Dafa, you are changing; as long as you read Dafa, you are elevating. The boundless content of Dafa plus the supplementary means—the exercises—will enable you to reach Consummation. Group reading or reading by yourself is the same.

The ancients have a saying, "Having heard the Dao in the morning, one can die in the evening." No one among mankind today can really understand its meaning. Did you know that when a person's mind accepts the Fa, that part of his mind that accepts the Fa is assimilated to the Fa? Where will that part go upon the death of that person who has heard the Fa? I ask you to study the Fa more, remove more attachments, and abandon various human notions, so that you will not take away with you only a certain part, but reach Consummation.

Li Hongzhi
August 3, 1998

The Buddha Fa and Buddhism

Many people think of Buddhism whenever Buddha is mentioned. Actually, Buddhism is only one form of the Buddha Fa's manifestations in the human world. The Buddha Fa also manifests itself in other ways in the human world. In other words, Buddhism cannot represent the entire Buddha Fa.

Not everything in Buddhism was taught by Buddha Sakyamuni. There are other forms of Buddhism in the world that do not revere Buddha Sakyamuni as their master. In fact, some have nothing to do with Buddha Sakyamuni. For example, what the Yellow Sect of Tibetan Buddhism worships is the Great Sun Tathagata, and it regards Buddha Sakyamuni as a Buddha Law Body of the Great Sun Tathagata. With Milerepa[25] as its object of worship, the White Sect of Tibetan Buddhism has nothing to do with Buddha Sakyamuni, nor does it mention Sakyamuni's Buddhism. Their believers during that time did not even know the name of Buddha Sakyamuni, let alone who Buddha Sakyamuni was. Other sects of Tibetan Buddhism have each understood Buddha Sakyamuni

---

[25] Milerepa—the founder of the White Sect of Tibetan Buddhism.

differently. Theravada has always regarded itself as the orthodox Buddhism taught by Buddha Sakyamuni, for it has indeed inherited, in terms of form, the cultivation method used in the era of Buddha Sakyamuni. It has kept the original precepts and dress, and it worships only Buddha Sakyamuni. Chinese Buddhism was altered before it was introduced in China. The cultivation method was altered drastically, with the worship of many Buddhas instead of Buddha Sakyamuni alone. In the meantime, the precepts have doubled in number and the rites of ancient China's civil religions have been incorporated. During their religious ceremonies, Chinese musical instruments—such as wooden fish, bells, gongs and drums—have been used, and they have changed the style of their clothes to that of ancient Chinese folk dress. It was renamed "Mahayana," and has become considerably different from Buddha Sakyamuni's early Buddhism. Therefore, Theravada at that time did not recognize Mahayana as Sakyamuni's Buddhism.

I mentioned the above in order to address the relationship between the Buddha Fa and Buddhism in the context of Buddhism. Now let me discuss it from a historical perspective. In Western society, among the unearthed relics of ancient Greek culture, the 卍 symbol was discovered. In fact, in the remote ages before Noah's Flood, people also worshipped Buddha. At the time of the Flood, some people of ancient Greek ancestry living in western Asia and the region to the southwest of the Himalayas survived. They were then called "Brahman," and they became today's White Indians. As a matter of fact, Brahmanism worshipped Buddha initially. It had inherited the tradition of revering Buddha from the ancient Greeks who, at that time, called Buddhas "gods." About a thousand years later, Brahmanism began its transfiguration, just like the alterations of Buddhism in modern Mahayana, the alterations in Tibetan Buddhism, the alterations in Japanese Buddhism, and so on. Over a thousand years after that in ancient India, Brahmanism began its Dharma-Ending period. People

100

started to worship crooked things rather than Buddha. At that time Brahman people no longer believed in Buddha. Instead, what they worshipped were all demons. Killing and sacrificing animals as ritual worship took place. By the time Buddha Sakyamuni was born, Brahmanism had already become a completely evil religion. This is not to say that Buddha had changed, but that the religion had become evil. Among the remaining cultural relics from ancient India, one can still find statues in the mountain caves from early Brahmanism. The carved statues of gods all resemble the images of Buddhas. They can also be found in Buddhism among the Buddha sculptures in China. For instance, in several major caves there are statues of two seated Buddhas facing each other, etc. Buddha was still Buddha—it was the religion that had become evil. Religion does not represent God(s) or Buddha. It was the depravity of the human heart that deformed the religion.

All of this shows that the Buddha Fa is eternal and that the Buddha Fa is the nature of the universe. It is the mighty Buddha Fa that creates Buddhas, and not Buddha Sakyamuni that created the Buddha Fa. Buddha Sakyamuni enlightened to the Buddha Fa, enlightening up to the level of his Attainment Status.

Let me make a few more remarks in terms of this cycle of human civilization. Did you know that Dao is one kind of god; Buddha is another kind of god; Yahweh, Jesus, and St. Mary are also one kind of god? Their Attainment Status and bodily forms vary as a result of differences in their cultivation objectives and in their understandings of the universe's Dafa. It is the Buddha Fa that created the immense cosmic body, and not these Buddhas, Daos, and Gods. This much is known to human beings. How much more remains unknown to mankind is still enormous! Didn't Buddha Sakyamuni once say that with respect to Tathagata Buddhas alone, they are as many as the grains of sand in the Ganges River? Could these Buddhas' teachings be the same as the Dharma taught by Buddha Sakyamuni? Could the teachings they would give, if and when they came to human society, match the Dharma taught by Buddha Sakyamuni word for word? Did the seven Buddhas before Buddha Sakyamuni teach the Dharma Buddha Sakyamuni taught? It is mentioned in Buddhism that the future Buddha, Buddha Maitreya, will come to this human world to preach his teachings. Will he then repeat Buddha Sakyamuni's words? I feel sad to find Buddhism today having reached this stage, being foolishly obsessed with religion itself rather than actually practicing cultivation. Hypocrites and religious scoundrels are seriously corrupting both the cultivation places and monks. On second thought, this is not so surprising. Buddha Sakyamuni actually once talked about the situation in the Dharma-Ending period. How different is modern Buddhism from Brahmanism in its later period?

At present, I come to this world to teach the Fa once again—to directly teach the fundamental Fa of the universe. Some people do not dare to admit this fact—not because they are concerned about their own cultivation, but rather for the purpose of protecting religion itself or because they allow their ordinary human emotions to get in the way. They equate religion with Buddha. There are others who object, using their ordinary human thinking, because their prominence in Buddhism is challenged. Is this a small attachment? Those with ulterior motives who dare to even slander the Buddha Fa and Buddhas, they have already become ghosts in hell. It is just that their lives on earth are not over yet. They always consider themselves to be some sort of religious scholars. Yet how much do they really know about the Buddha Fa! Oftentimes, as soon as Buddha is mentioned, they will immediately relate it to Buddhism; as soon as the Buddha School is mentioned, they will think that it is the Buddhism of their denomination; as soon as the Buddha Fa is mentioned, they will regard it as what they know.

There are many people around the world who practice cultivation deep in the mountains for a long time. Many of them practice cultivation by following different cultivation ways in the Buddha School, which have been passed down for hundreds of years. They have nothing to do with Sakyamuni's religion. For those religious scoundrels who are not even clear about these concepts or terms, what kind of qualifications do they have to criticize Falun Dafa? In the past, Jesus's appearance upset Judaism. Two thousand five hundred years ago, Sakyamuni's appearance shook Brahmanism. It seems that people can never learn positive lessons from history. Instead, they always learn from negative lessons for the sake of their own self-interests. In the universe, there is the law of formation, settlement, and deterioration. Nothing is constant and without change. There are Buddhas in different historical periods who come to this world to save people. History develops in this way. Mankind in the future will also hear of the Buddha Fa.

Li Hongzhi
December 17, 1998

Dafa Cannot be Used

Dafa can save all beings. Standing before the great facts, even those so-called "high-level beings" who are escaping into the Three Realms and those from the Three Realms who have done damage to Dafa can no longer deny it. Even so, a problem has come along and manifest itself among ordinary humans. For example, some people who used to oppose Dafa or did not believe in Dafa have also come to learn to practice Dafa cultivation. Dafa can save all beings. I do not object to anyone coming to learn it, and in fact I have been teaching Dafa to all beings. The key point is that deep down inside, these people do not regard me as their true master. Their purpose for learning Dafa is to use it to protect things deep down inside that they cannot let go of, things in religion, or God. This is an act of plagiarizing the Fa. The intention of taking advantage of Dafa is itself an unforgivable sin. For some of them, however, the human side of their minds is not quite so aware; therefore, I have been observing them all along. Because I think that, regardless of the reason they have taken up the path of Dafa, it is still a rare opportunity for them—I am giving wrongdoers another chance. After all, he or she was born into a time when Dafa is being spread widely, and he or she is also in a human body. I have been waiting for them to come to realize this.

There is actually also a group of people who came like this and have completely changed their original understanding, becoming determined, genuine Dafa disciples. But there is still another group of people who do not intend to change and who have long been stumbling along in Dafa. For the sake of Dafa's stability in the human world, I cannot condone their continuing any further. Thus, they will really miss their chance. As I said, superficial changes are for others to see. Whether or not you can be saved depends on the change and ascension of your own heart. If change does not occur there, you cannot improve and nothing can be achieved. Actually, it is because of reading *Zhuan Falun* that your body has been somewhat blessed on the surface. Other than that, you have not attained anything. With a mind that ill, could you attain anything else? Human beings! Think about it! What should you believe? What shouldn't you believe? Why do you practice cultivation? For whom do you practice cultivation? For whom does your life exist? I trust that you will weigh such questions properly. Otherwise, you will never be able to make up for what you will lose. When Dafa reveals itself to mankind, these are not the only things that you will lose.

Li Hongzhi
March 16, 1999

Determination and Solidity

The Buddha Fa cultivation practice is majestic. At the same time, it is also serious. Disciples, you only know that there exist truth and falsehood in the secular world, but you do not know that lives in other dimensions—including gods—vary greatly throughout the universe, due to their different levels. This leads to differences in their understandings of things and of the truth. In particular, due to the circumstance that they are unclear about the reality regarding the Fa-rectification, some have caused severe interference and resistance, doing damage by using different methods to come into contact with students. They have thereby caused some practitioners who have their Third Eye opened at low levels to have doubts and confusion about Dafa. Among these beings within the Three Realms (the so-called "gods") and the various so-called "high-level beings" who have fled over from higher dimensions in order to escape the Fa-rectification, most of them do not know the truth regarding the Fa-rectification and resist the Fa-rectification itself. They are undermining the students' upstanding faith and determination by exhibiting or telling the practitioners some of their understandings based on their own notions, or by imparting some things to the students, and so on. Actually, those are all very low level things and are deceptive lies. Since they are gods, they appear to be very kind, causing groups of students who

105

have insufficient understanding of Dafa to develop thoughts of wavering. Consequently, some people have stopped studying Dafa, and some have even gone to the opposite side. At present, this problem is very serious. Because of this, these people's situation is extremely lamentable. At the same time, they will never regain what they have lost, and this is a huge disaster in their life.

I have already mentioned all of this to you in *Essentials for Further Advancement* and in *Zhuan Falun*, in the topics: "no second cultivation way," and "how to practice cultivation with your Third Eye open." Why can't you handle yourself properly once you see those so-called "higher beings," who feign kindness, talking to you? Can they have you reach Consummation? Why don't you think about it? Why did they ignore you before you learned Dafa? Why have they become so concerned about you after you have learned Dafa? Cultivation is serious. I have already taught you all the principles of the Fa. All of these things are something that you have to go through and tests that you have to pass in your personal cultivation practice. Failing to pass them is your own doing. All this time I have been giving you opportunities to realize this and to get back on track. For the sake of Dafa, I could not wait any longer and had to write this article. I know that when you read this article you are bound to be awakened; but this does not come from your own cultivation. Why haven't others been interfered with? I have said that the Fa-rectification started from outside of the Three Realms, and therefore some so-called "gods" within the Three Realms could not see it. Thus, they dared to do things that harmed Dafa. When the Fa-rectification entered the Three Realms and the human world, they had nowhere to escape to. However, there are records of everything they have done, which then become the future positions that they place themselves into. Some will lower their levels, and some will become human beings. Some will become ghosts in the netherworld, and some will be completely destroyed through almost endless and repeated destruction as payment for all that they have done; this is because those are the positions that they get through the most truthful exhibition of their own *xinxing*. This way, all lives from above are also rearranging their positions in Dafa, not to mention these things in the human world and its ordinary human beings. In the Fa-rectification, there are those who ascend, there are those who descend, and there are those who are destroyed. Regardless of whether they are gods, humans, or ghosts, all will be placed anew in one of the positions in different realms—from survival to total elimination. You human beings are treasured because you are able to practice cultivation; that is why you are taught such high-level principles. You are treasured because through cultivation you are capable of becoming truly great enlightened beings with virtuous enlightenment and righteous Fa.

Li Hongzhi
March 16, 1999

Purge Demon-Nature

In the wake of the Western U.S. Dafa Experience Sharing Conference, some people who listened to the Fa with attachments claimed that cultivation practice would soon come to an end and that Master would leave, taking a portion of practitioners with him. This is an act that seriously damages Dafa, and it is a massive exposure of demon-nature. When did I ever make such statements? This comes from your understanding things wrong due to your attachments. How do you know that you will achieve Consummation? How could you achieve Consummation when you are not even able to let go of your own attachments? Dafa is serious. How could it follow what evil religions do? What other forms of demon-nature do you still harbor? Why do you have to switch to the opposite side of Dafa? If you still want to be my disciples, immediately stop being used by demons when you are talking.

Disciples, I have said repeatedly that cultivation practice is both serious and sacred. At the same time, our cultivation should be responsible to society, mankind, and ourselves. Why can't you practice cultivation nobly and in a way that conforms to the society of everyday people? For all those who told others that there was no time left, that they were making their final arrangements, or that the Master would leave and take so-and-so with him, and so on, I suggest that you immediately undo the impact that you have either directly or indirectly caused. Not even one sentence should be taken advantage of by demons. Our way of achieving Consummation must be open and aboveboard.

Li Hongzhi
March 30, 1999

True Nature Revealed

Firmly cultivate Dafa with an unaffected heart and mind,

Raising one's level is fundamental,

In the face of trials, one's true nature is revealed,

Achieve Consummation, becoming a Buddha, Dao or God.

Li Hongzhi
May 8, 1999

Some Thoughts of Mine

Recently it was reported in the news that Mainland China seeks a reduction of US$500 million worth of trade surplus (with the U.S.) in exchange for my extradition back to China. I would like to make some comments on this matter. I only teach people to be good. At the same time, I unconditionally help people eliminate their illnesses, and I enable them to reach higher realms of mind. I do not accept any monetary or material reward. All this has had a positive impact on society and mankind, bringing goodness to people's hearts and dignity to human morality. Are these the reasons why they seek to extradite me? Do they intend to have me return to China to let more people obtain the Fa and cultivate their hearts and minds? If that is the case, please do not let the country lose US$500 million to strike a deal. I can go back myself.

I have heard, however, that normally the people who are extradited are war criminals, public enemies, or criminal offenders. If so, I do not know into which of the above categories I would be placed.

As a matter of fact, I keep teaching people to conduct themselves according to the guiding principles of Zhen-Shan-Ren. So naturally I have also been setting an example. During the times when Falun Gong disciples and I, myself, were being discredited for no reason and being treated unfairly, we always exhibited hearts of great compassion and tolerance and endured all of it silently, so as to give the government sufficient time to understand us. Nevertheless, such tolerance is absolutely not because Falun Gong practitioners and I fear anything. It should be known that once a person learns the truth and the real meaning of life, he will not regret giving up his life for that. Do not take our hearts of compassion and great tolerance as fear, and double the efforts in doing whatever you want. In fact, those are enlightened practitioners, and they are cultivators who have learned the true meaning of life. Also, do not label Falun Gong practitioners as people who engage in alleged "superstition." There are so many things that mankind and science have not yet come to understand. As far as religions are concerned, don't they also exist as a result of faith in gods? In reality, it is only the genuine religions and ancient beliefs in gods that have enabled the morality of human society to be maintained for several thousand years, making the existence of today's mankind—which includes you, me, him, etc.—possible. If this were not the case, mankind would have committed sins long ago that would have led to catastrophes. Humans' ancestors probably would have become extinct long ago, and today's events would never have occurred. Human morality is, in fact, extremely important. If people do not value virtue, they can commit all kinds of wrongdoing that are extremely dangerous to mankind. This is what I can tell people. Actually, I have no intention of doing anything for society, nor do I wish to get involved in ordinary human matters at all, let alone take power away from anybody. Not everyone considers power to be so important. Isn't there a saying among mankind that "everyone has his own will"? I only wish to let those who can practice cultivation obtain the Fa, as well as to teach them how to truly improve their *xinxing*; that is, to improve their moral standards. Furthermore, not everyone will come to learn Falun Gong. Also, what I am doing is bound to have no connection with politics. Yet, for any country or nationality it is a good thing to have cultivators whose hearts have embraced benevolence and whose levels of morality have improved. How can it be labeled an evil religion for helping people to heal their sicknesses and stay healthy, while raising human moral standards? Every Falun Gong practitioner is a member of society, and each has his or her own job or career. They simply go to the parks to do Falun Gong exercises for half an hour to an hour every morning, then go off to work. We have no required religious regulations of any kind, nor are there any temples, churches, or religious rituals. People can come to learn it, or leave as they please—there is no binding membership. In what way does it have anything to do with religion? As to the label "evil," how could it fall into the category of "evil" for teaching people to be benevolent, healing people's sicknesses, and keeping them healthy, all without accepting any money? Or should something be considered evil if it is outside the category of communist theories? Besides, I know that evil religion is just evil religion, and it is not up to a government to decide. Should an evil religion be called "upright" if it conforms to the views of some people in government? On the other hand, should an upright one be defined as evil if it does not conform to their views?

Actually, I know exactly why some people insist on opposing Falun Gong. Just as reported by the media, there are too many people practicing Falun Gong. A hundred million people is indeed no small number. Yet why should having too many good people be feared? Isn't it true that the more good people there are, the better, while the fewer bad people there are, the better? I, Li Hongzhi, unconditionally help practitioners improve their moral quality and keep people healthy, and this in turn stabilizes society. Moreover, with their bodies healthy, people can better serve society. Isn't this bringing good fortune to the people in power? In reality, this has indeed been achieved. Why, instead of recognizing this or showing me appreciation, do they want to estrange more than 100 million people from the government? What kind of government would be so inconceivable? Furthermore, who among these 100 million people doesn't have a family and children, or relatives and friends? Is it merely an issue of 100 million people? So the number of people they are going against could be even more. "What on earth has happened to the leadership of my beloved country?" If I, with the life of Li Hongzhi, can dispel the fear towards these good people, I

111

will go back at once and leave everything to their disposal. Why bother with "going against the will of the law under heaven," wasting manpower and capital, and using politics and money to seek a deal that violates human rights? The United States, on the other hand, has been a leader in respecting human rights. Given this, how could the U.S. government be willing to betray human rights for a deal like this? In addition, I am a U.S. permanent resident who lives under the jurisdiction of U.S. law.

I do not intend to condemn any particular person. It is just that I do not understand the way things are being handled. Why miss a good opportunity to appeal to the people's hearts, instead placing more than 100 million people on the opposing side?

It was reported that many people went to Zhongnanhai,[26] and that some people were outraged by this. In fact, the number of people who went there was not large at all. Think about it, everyone: There are over 100 million people practicing Falun Gong, and only over ten thousand people showed up. How can that be considered a large number? There was no need to mobilize practitioners. Among 100 million practitioners, since you wanted to go and he wanted to go, in a short while, over ten thousand people would be there. They did not have any slogans or any signs, nor was there any improper conduct. Furthermore, they were not opposing the government. They merely wished to present the facts to the government. What was wrong with that? Please allow me to ask: Have there ever been such well-behaved demonstrators? Shouldn't one be moved by such a sight? Why do some people keep trying to find fault with Falun Gong? Besides, the approach taken in resorting to any and all means in order to eliminate Falun Gong is really outdated.

---

[26] Zhongnanhai (jong-nahn-high)—the Chinese leadership compound, located in Beijing; it houses the Appeals Office of the State Department.

Falun Gong is not terrible, as some people might have imagined it to be. Instead, it is a wonderful thing. Any society has everything to gain from it and nothing to lose, while losing people's hearts, on the other hand, is the most frightening thing. To be frank, the practitioners of Falun Gong are also human beings who are in the process of practicing cultivation, so they still have human minds. Since they are being treated unjustly, I am not sure how much longer they will be able to endure it. This is the matter I am most concerned about.

Li Hongzhi
June 2, 1999

Position

The trials that practitioners go through are trials that everyday people could not bear. Therefore, those in history who were able to succeed in cultivation and reach Consummation were few and far between. Human beings are just human beings. On critical occasions it is very hard for them to abandon their human thinking, and they always find excuses to justify themselves. A great cultivator, however, is able to let go of his ego and all his ordinary human thinking in the midst of crucial tests. I congratulate those Dafa cultivators who have made it through the tests that determine whether they can achieve Consummation. The eternity in which your lives are unending and the level where you will be in the future—these you establish yourselves. Mighty virtues are cultivated by you, yourselves. So strive forward. This is the greatest and most magnificent thing.

Li Hongzhi
June 13, 1999

Stability

The events that occurred a short time ago have already caused many Falun Dafa practitioners serious harm. At the same time, these events have also severely tarnished the nation's image. Based on what students know regarding how the relevant regions or the relevant departments directly or covertly interfered with and disrupted the practice sessions of Falun Gong students, students can report these cases through the usual channels to the various levels of the government or the country's leadership. As for the situation whereby some people used the power that they held to instigate the Falun Gong incident—putting a broad segment of the people and government in opposition to each other as an opportunity to seize political capital—students may also report this through the usual channels to the various levels of the government or to the country's leadership.

We are cultivators, however. Do not participate in politics and do not be disturbed by these previous events. Calm your hearts and minds, resume your normal practice, study the Fa, strive forward, and cultivate solidly, constantly improving yourselves.

Li Hongzhi
June 13, 1999

Further Comments on Superstition (*Mi Xin*)

Initially, "superstition" was just an ordinary term. Some people in political circles in China hyped it into a term with deadly power. Actually, superstition as publicized by those in political circles is not superstition, but a political label and a political slogan; it is a political term used specifically when attacking others. Once something is slapped with this label, it is made antithetical to science and can thus be blatantly attacked.

In fact, those who have gone through different kinds of political movements possess really strong analytical abilities. In the past, they had beliefs, disappointments, and blind worship, and they learned their lessons from these experiences. In particular, they experienced an unforgettable blow to their souls during the Cultural Revolution. How could it be possible for these people to casually believe in anything? People today are the most capable of distinguishing clearly whether something is the truth or so-called "superstition" cooked up by political people.

Whether something is science or superstition is not to be decided by people involved in politics. Instead, it should be appraised by scientists. Yet the so-called "scientists" being used for political purposes are actually political figures as well. It is impossible for these kinds of people to genuinely draw a fair and scientific conclusion from an objective, scientific standpoint. This being the case, they cannot be called scientists whatsoever. At most, they can only serve as a club held in the hands of politicians and be used to strike at people.

The understanding of the truth of the universe by students of Dafa cultivation results from their elevation through reason and experience. It is futile for man, regardless of what perspective he takes, to refute the Fa and principles of the universe, which are beyond all theories of human society—especially when the morality of human society is on the verge of total collapse and the mighty universe has once again shown great compassion and given mankind this final chance. Mankind should treasure and cherish this hope above all. Out of selfish desires, however, man is undermining this last hope the universe has granted him, thereby incurring the wrath of the entire universe. Even so, ignorant people take various catastrophes as natural phenomena. The universe does not exist for mankind. Man is only one form of expression of life, existing at the lowest level. If mankind fails to meet the standard for existence at this level of the universe, it can only be eliminated by the universe's history.

Mankind! Wake up! The vows of gods throughout the ages are being fulfilled. Dafa is evaluating all lives. The path of life is under one's own feet. A person's own single thought will also determine his future.

Treasure and cherish it: The Fa and the principles of the universe are right in front of you.

Li Hongzhi
July 13, 1999